get hooked

SIMPLE STEPS TO CROCHET COOL STUFF

by Kim Werker

Photography by ANGELA FAMA
and PAMELA BETHEL

Illustrations by CYNTHIA FRENETTE

WATSON-GUPTILL PUBLICATIONS/NEW YORK

Senior Acquisitions Editor: Julie Mazur
Editor: Linda Hetzer
Designer: Margo Mooney
Senior Production Manager: Ellen Greene

First published in 2006 by Watson-Guptill Publications,
a division of VNU Business Media, Inc.,
770 Broadway, New York, NY 10003
www.wgpub.com

Library of Congress Control Number: 2005939000

ISBN-10: 0-8230-5092-0
ISBN-13: 978-0-8230-5092-5

Printed in China

First printing, 2006

1 2 3 4 5 6 7 8 9 / 14 13 12 11 10 09 08 07 06

dedication

To DLP, who rises to the occasion.
And to summer camps, where the magic happens.
In memory of EL.

acknowledgments

The designers who contributed to this book are so wildly talented. Huge thanks to them for making this book possible, and for their dedication to the craft of crochet. Thanks, also, to the yarn companies who so generously and on such short notice supplied the materials to make the projects.

To my editors Julie Mazur and Linda Hetzer, thank you for your vision, your patience, and your creativity. Huge thanks to Julie Holetz for expert technical editing, great advice, and growing friendship. Cynthia Frenette's illustrations make the world a happier place, and Margo Mooney's design can't be beat. Angela Fama's and Pam Bethel's photos make crochet look as cool as it is, and I thank them for a wicked amount of photo shoot fun. Big hugs to the models who fill these pages with their happy faces.

A big shout-out to Shannon, who's never short of humor and who always has an even huger idea in the wings. Thanks to my parents for their support and enthusiasm and to my grandmother and my zayde, the poet. Thanks to my extended in-law family, too, for matching encouragement, and to Cleo, my furry friend. Most of all, thanks to Greg for being my partner, always, and for making me feel talented and loved.

contents

Introduction

WHY CROCHET? What's so cool about making stuff with yarn? Well, to begin with, it's fun and relaxing and exciting and creative and interesting. And everyone's doing it! I mean, have you opened a magazine lately? Crochet's everywhere, from ball gown trims to hot bikinis, to jewelry, shrugs, capelets, and hats and scarves.

Sure, you could go to the mall or your favorite boutique to buy crocheted stuff. But what's the fun in that? When you make it yourself, you can choose the perfect colors, make the perfect fit, and have a great time while you're at it. And it's likely you can do it more affordably, too.

All you need to start crocheting is yarn and a crochet hook. (The word *crochet* means "hook" in French. Who knew? All this time we've been calling it a *hook* hook!) This means your project is totally portable. Take it on the bus or the subway, to the park, or to a friend's house. You can crochet during your lunch break, while you're watching TV, and when you're hanging out with friends. Some people even feel like they concentrate better when they're crocheting!

Speaking of your friends—how much will they love it when you can make them totally personalized gifts? Hello?! Start planning for the holidays now! Better yet, learn to crochet along with a few friends and you can swap cool gifts all year round.

Really, crochet is just fun. Work on a simple project when you want to relax and let your mind wander. As you get better and better at it, your hands will start to move without you trying so hard, and you'll be able to totally zone out for a while. Pick a more involved project when you want to learn new skills and feel really proud of your accomplishment. The great thing about crochet is that mistakes are super easy to correct, so there's no pressure to get it exactly right the first time around.

So, are you convinced? Good. Let's get started.

hooked yet?

Crochet is addictive, isn't it? I bet you're tempted to do it for hours and hours at a time. Just remember to be careful! Crocheting involves small, repetitive motions that can actually hurt you if you don't take it easy. So take frequent breaks—for at least 15 minutes each time. Stretch your fingers and rotate your wrists to keep them flexible and moving smoothly. If you feel any pain at all, put down your hook immediately and talk to an adult. Crocheting is great fun so make sure you keep those hands and fingers in good shape!

gotta get it

Hooks, yarn, and notions—the stuff of crochet. Learn about the tools and materials you need to have a great time crocheting, and try to gather them in advance to avoid a mad rush when you start your first project!

A Hook

You only need one crochet hook to get started! But after a while you'll find it's a good idea to have several hooks around, and here's why.

Hooks are made from many different materials and come in many sizes (though they're pretty much all shaped like hooks, obviously). Hooks are most commonly made of plastic, aluminum, bamboo, or wood.

The smallest hooks, used to crochet thin threads, are made of steel. You'll want to experiment with different kinds of hooks so you can find the ones you like the best. You may find you prefer to use one type of hook with a particular yarn—such as bamboo hooks with cotton yarn or plastic hooks with wool. You'll also want hooks in a variety of sizes so you're ready to work with lots of different yarn weights.

your comfort zone

Hook handles, especially on steel hooks, can be very thin, and your hand may get tired or sore from doing lots of crocheting with it. Keep an eye out for hooks that have nice, wide grips—just like pens and pencils, the wider the grip, the happier your hand will be. If you can't find thick-handled hooks, you can always make some yourself. What I like to do is put a rubber pencil grip on my hook. If the hook's too narrow for the grip to stay in place, wrap medical tape around the hook to widen it before putting on the grip.

A LOOK AT SHAPE

There are two things that make a hook appropriate for a certain weight of yarn (more on yarn weight a little later)—the depth of the hook and the width of the shaft.

The width of the shaft determines the size of the crochet hook. The wider the diameter of the shaft, the larger your stitches will be, and the heavier weight yarn you can use comfortably with the hook. The narrower the shaft, the smaller your stitches will be and the finer the yarn you can use.

You should be able to grab the yarn with your hook easily and reliably. If your yarn keeps slipping away from your hook, try a different hook. Different brands shape their hooks differently, so experiment until you find a hook shape that works for you.

HOOK

THROAT

SHAFT

GRIP

HANDLE

which hand?

ost people hold their hook in the same hand they write with, but try using your other hand, too, to see which one is more comfortable. Your hook hand moves the hook in and out of stitches, but your other hand plays an important role, too! It controls the yarn that's fed to your hook, and it keeps the tension regular so that your stitches come out even.

A LOOK AT SIZE

Hooks come in many sizes. Unfortunately, there isn't a universal standard for how to label these sizes. In North America, you'll find hooks sized in one of two systems: the metric system or the American system. The metric system is based on the actual measurement, in millimeters, of the diameter of the hook's shaft. In the American system, sizes of most hooks are given in letters, and the smaller steel hook sizes are given in numbers (but the numbers don't correspond to a measurement). The American system is pretty arbitrary, and there isn't always a direct relationship between the American size and the metric size. Different brands might even give the same metric-sized hook a different letter! It's confusing, but the chart at the right can help you out.

For each project in this book, the required hook size is listed in metric first, followed by the American size in parentheses—for example, 6.5mm (size K) crochet hook.

Steel hooks, which are the littler ones used for fine threads, range in size from 0.75mm (size 14) to 3.5mm (size 00). They are usually used for cotton threads of all weights and for fingering weight yarn. A steel crochet hook is used with cotton embroidery floss to make the Friendship Cuffs (see page 72). Non-steel crochet hooks range in size from 2.25mm (size B) to 19.0mm (size S), or larger.

Hook Sizes

METRIC SIZE	AMERICAN SIZE	STEEL HOOK SIZE
0.75mm		14
0.85mm		13
1.0mm		12
1.1mm		11
1.3mm		10
1.4mm		9
1.5mm		8
1.65mm		7
1.8mm		6
1.9mm		5
2.0mm		4
2.1mm		3
2.25mm	B	2
2.75mm	C	1
3.25mm	D	0
3.5mm	E	00
3.75mm	F	
4.0mm	G	
4.5mm		
5.0mm	H	
5.5mm	I	
6.0mm	J	
6.5mm	K	
7.0mm		
8.0mm	L	
9.0mm	M/N	
10.0mm	N/P	
15.0mm	P/Q	
16.0mm	Q	
19.0mm	S	

tip

When you first start crocheting, you might find that you make your stitches too tight. If you do, just use a larger hook. When you get a better feel for how to make the stitches, you'll start crocheting more loosely and can go back to using a smaller hook.

Yarn

Yarn is what makes the crochet world go round. Yarn is made in many fibers, constructions, and weights, so let's take a look at each.

FIBER Yarn can be made of two kinds of fiber: natural and synthetic. **Natural** fibers come from animals (such as sheep, alpacas, silkworms, and angora rabbits) or plants (such as cotton, soy, and hemp). **Synthetic** fibers are made from chemicals, and include acrylic, polyester, and nylon. Natural fibers can be more expensive than synthetics, and they tend to be warm and breathable, but require gentle hand washing. Synthetic fibers come in a vast array of textures and colors, and are generally easier to care for than natural fibers, as they can often be machine washed. Many yarns are blends of natural and synthetic fibers, and benefit from the qualities of both.

CONSTRUCTION Yarn can also be divided into two general constructions: traditional and novelty. **Traditional** yarns are what come to mind when you hear the word "yarn." They're generally smooth and are sometimes plied (two or more thinner strands of yarn are twisted together to make a thicker, stronger strand). **Novelty** yarns have funky textures, such as fun fur, chenille, boucle, ribbon, and more. As a beginner, you should stick to traditional yarns for your first few projects. These yarns will show your stitches clearly, which will help you count stitches and find any mistakes. Once you're comfortable with the basics you can play with novelty yarns all you want!

WEIGHT Another way to categorize yarns is by their weight, from **super fine** to **super bulky.** The thinner the yarn, the smaller the hook you use, and the bulkier the yarn, the larger the hook. Take a look at the chart (opposite) for a description of different yarn weights.

Although most patterns specify a particular yarn, you can easily substitute a different one. Just make sure you use a yarn of the same weight and that you crochet to the same gauge listed in the pattern (more on gauge later, too).

The Craft Yarn Council of America's Standard Yarn Weight System

YARN WEIGHT CATEGORY	SYMBOL	TYPES OF YARN	HOW MANY SINGLE CROCHET STITCHES IN 4 INCHS?	RECOMMENDED HOOK SIZES (U.S.)	RECOMMENDED HOOK SIZES (METRIC)
Super fine	**1** SUPER FINE	Sock, fingering, baby	21–32 stitches	B to E	2.25–3.5 mm
Fine	**2** FINE	Sport, baby	16–20 stitches	E to G	3.5–4.5 mm
Light	**3** LIGHT	DK, light worsted	12–17 stitches	G to I	4.5–5.5 mm
Medium	**4** MEDIUM	Worsted, afghan, aran	11–14 stitches	I to K	5.5–6.5 mm
Bulky	**5** BULKY	Chunky, craft, rug	8–11 stitches	K to M	6.5–9 mm
Super bulky	**6** SUPER BULKY	Bulky, roving	5–9 stitches	M and larger	9mm and larger

This chart shows how yarn is put into categories by weight. If you like a pattern but want to switch the yarn, you can usually choose another one in the same weight category.

yarn online

𝒴ou can check out a particular yarn—and all the colors it comes in!—on most yarn company's websites (see page 94). You can also order yarn online at a ton of online yarn stores or even on eBay. Just do a search for "yarn," or even "blue angora yarn," and you might find a terrific deal!

SHOPPING FOR YARN

When you buy yarn, it comes packaged in one of three ways.

A **ball** is spherical. You use the yarn by unraveling the ball from the outside.

A **skein** is more of a cylinder. You use the yarn either by unraveling it from the outside, or by fishing around in the center of the skein and finding the other end. It's usually easier to pull the yarn from the center of a skein.

A **hank** is a loosely wound quantity of yarn. It needs to be rewound into a ball before you use it, or it will tangle almost immediately and be impossible to use. The most fun way to wind a hank into a ball is to have a friend or family member wrap the hank around her forearms. Then you can unwrap the yarn from her arms and wind it into a ball. Start by winding the yarn several times around your first two fingers. Then remove the yarn from your fingers and continue to wind the yarn around itself, changing directions every so often so you end up with a ball. If you're winding a ball of yarn yourself, try sitting on the floor with the hank around your feet or knees, or putting the hank around the back of a chair or even around your neck.

Have a friend hold the hank of yarn while you wind it into a ball.

tip

If you're using yarn from a ball, put it in a zipper-lock plastic bag. Pull out the strand of yarn and close the bag most of the way. Now you can keep the bag next to you and pull the yarn out without the ball rolling all over the place!

Shown left to right: a skein (green), a ball (blue), and a hank (fuschia).

READING A YARN LABEL

Most yarn comes wrapped in a label that tells you everything you need to know about the yarn.

QUANTITY You'll see how much the skein weighs (in ounces and/or grams) and how much yarn it contains (in yards and/or meters). This information is very important when it comes to figuring out how many balls of yarn you'll need to buy, especially if you're substituting the yarn called for in the pattern.

FIBER CONTENT The label tells you what kind(s) of fibers the yarn is made from and in what proportion.

DYE LOT When yarn is dyed, it is given a dye lot number. If you are making a large item that calls for several skeins of yarn, be sure to buy skeins with the same dye number. This means they were dyed together in the same batch.

RECOMMENDED HOOK SIZE Since each person crochets differently—more loosely or tightly—remember that the hook size called for on a yarn label is only a suggestion. If the label only has a recommendation for knitting needle size, use a crochet hook that's the same metric size as the needles.

CARE INSTRUCTIONS The label explains how to wash items made from the yarn, usually in symbols. For example, the symbols on this label indicate, from left to right, that items should be hand washed, should not be bleached, and should be dried flat. Don't ignore these instructions; you want to take good care of the project you spent so much time (and money) on!

MANUFACTURER'S NAME

Yummy Yarns

Dreamy Delight — YARN NAME

FIBER CONTENT — **50% Cotton/50% Wool**

**5 oz./140 g.
Approximate Length
153 yards/140 meters** — WEIGHT AND LENGTH

Cherry Red — YARN COLOR
DYE LOT NUMBER — **Lot: 3047**

Gauge: — GAUGE
**14 stitches/18 rows = 4 inches
Needle size: 10
10 sc stitches/11 rows = 4 inches
Hook size: K/6.5 mm**

CARE INSTRUCTIONS

CHOOSING COLORS

Yarn comes in as many colors as ice cream does flavors—and it's just as yummy. Feeling so happy you can't contain yourself? Make something yellow, orange, and pink. Feeling a little down? Crochet something blue. Making a gift for an outdoorsy guy? Use browns and grays. Looking for a baby gift? Skip the usual pastels and make a bright green baby hat!

Your choice of color can make the same pattern look entirely different. In this book, we list the yarn colors that were used to create the projects shown in the photographs. But you don't have to use those exact colors! One of the easiest ways to be creative with crochet is to substitute your favorite colors for the ones in the pattern. You can use exactly the same yarn in a different color, and your project will be that much more an expression of who you are.

What colors should you choose? Take a look around and you'll find color inspiration everywhere. Make an autumn scarf in colors taken from the leaves outside your house in the fall—or make the same scarf in light blue and white and wear it skiing! Check out the veggies at the grocery store, your favorite video game, magazines, stuff you painted when you were a little kid…the possibilities are truly endless.

You can be very technical about choosing colors by using a color wheel to see which colors go nicely together. Or you can fly by the seat of your pants and just go with what you like. In either case, remember that there are no rules about color. If you don't like what you made, you can always start over!

Notions

In addition to yarn and some hooks, it's a good idea to keep a few other tools handy to help you work on your projects quickly and neatly. These items can be found at almost any craft store and at all good yarn stores.

Stitch markers allow you to mark a place in your project. Crochet stitch markers are different from knitting stitch markers, so if you buy them at the store, make sure you get the right ones. Crochet stitch markers are placed directly into the stitch, so you have to be able to open them. Avoid using safety pins that have a coil, because the yarn can get stuck in the coil and break or shred.

A **tape measure** is used to, well, take measurements! Use it to find out what size hat, gloves, skirt, or top you want to make. You can also use a tape measure to check your gauge (see page 33 for more on gauge).

A **yarn needle** (sometimes called a **tapestry needle**) is thicker than a sewing needle, has a blunt tip, and has a bigger eye to accommodate thicker yarns. Use a yarn needle to weave in stray yarn tails when you've finished a project and to sew seams together with yarn.

Scissors require no explanation. They're always handy.

A **row counter** is used to keep track of how many rows you've crocheted. You may find it helpful to have one with your supplies.

A **calculator** isn't just for math class! Once you get the hang of crochet, use a calculator to help you adjust a pattern so it works perfectly with the size of your stitches and the yarn you've chosen.

tip
If you don't have commercial stitch markers handy, try using a hoop earring!

Clockwise from top left: Yarn needle, calculator, tape measure, scissors, stitch markers.

Reading Patterns

Crochet patterns are simply instructions for how to make something. They may look intimidating, but just start at the beginning and go step by step.

At the very beginning of a pattern you'll find information about the things you need—yarn, hook size, notions, and anything else. There's also information about the size of the finished project (that's especially important if you're making a garment) and also about gauge (more about that on page 33).

Then there's the pattern itself. Read through the entire pattern once or twice before you start so you have a clear idea of what you'll need to do. Take a good look at the schematic drawings, too, so you get a good feel for how the piece is constructed. Also, be sure to check out the directions for finishing up, and study any special stitches that are used—you might even want to practice a new stitch with an extra piece of yarn.

Patterns are generally written as a set of row-by-row (when you are making rectangles) or round-by-round (when you are making circles) instructions. Each publication has its own style, but the general approach is the same. If there is a group of stitches that is repeated several times across one row or round, it will be placed between **asterisks** (* *) and referred to as "Repeat from * to * X number of times." For example, "*Single crochet in the next 2 stitches, double crochet in the next stitch* to end of row" means that you should single crochet in each of the next two stitches, then double crochet in the next stitch, over and over, until you reach the end of the row.

ready to start?

If you're new to crochet, there are three projects in the book that use only the basic stitches and techniques: the **Chunky Scarf** on page 34, the **Fresh-Face Washcloth** on page 42, and the **Hipster Head Scarf** on page 50. You might want to begin with one of these because the directions are extra-simple and the projects are quick to make.

Brackets (straight or curvy) and **parentheses** are also used to help make the pattern easier to understand. Sometimes several stitches are made into the same stitch from the previous row or round. So if you see instructions that say something like "Work [double crochet, treble crochet, double crochet] into the next stitch," it means that all three stitches are made into the same stitch from the previous row or round.

If a pattern uses more than one color of yarn, the colors are indicated as **Color A, Color B,** and so on.

The patterns in this book are written out in full sentences, but most crochet patterns are written in crochet shorthand (like **sc** for **single crochet**). That's because crochet directions can get pretty long, and using shorthand enables the patterns to be as short and concise as possible. Take a look at the chart opposite that lists common abbreviations, and you'll have no trouble diving right into other patterns.

Abbreviations

ABBREVIATION	TRANSLATION
approx	approximately
beg	begin/beginning
bet	between
blo or BLO	back loop only
CC	contrasting color
ch(s) or CH(S)	chain(s)
ch sp or CH-SP or ch-sp	chain space
cont	continue/continuing
dc or DC	double crochet
dec or DEC	decrease/decreasing
flo or FLO	front loop only
hdc or HDC	half double crochet
hk or HK	hook
inc or INC	increase/increasing
lp(s) or LP(S)	loop(s)
MC	main color
pat or patt	pattern
pm or PM	place marker
prev	previous
rem	remain/remaining
rnd(s) or RND(S)	round(s)
sc or SC	single crochet
sl st or Sl St or SS	slip stitch
st(s) or ST(S)	stitch(es)
tog or TOG	together
tr or TR	treble (triple) crochet
yo or YO	yarn over

step by step

From how to hold your hook to how to finish off a piece, and all the stitches in between—this chapter will make a crocheter out of you. It's time to dive in!

What Is Crochet?

Crochet is the process of interlocking loops of yarn. It's that simple. All you need is yarn and a crochet hook!

Here's the basic way crochet works: You start by making a number of simple, connected stitches called **chains,** which make up a **foundation chain** (see pages 23–24). Once you have your foundation chain, you make your first row of crochet stitches into its loops, and then you make row after row of stitches on top of it. (If you're following a pattern, it will tell you exactly what to do.)

There are a ton of stitches you can use in crochet—each creates a different look. This book will teach you the basic ones, but there are lots more you can learn if you want. Try these first, then explore some others!

smooth moves

Getting comfortable with crochet means getting comfortable with three basic moves that are done in a continuous motion—inserting the hook into a loop or stitch, wrapping the yarn around the hook (called a **yarn over**), and then pulling the yarn through the loop.

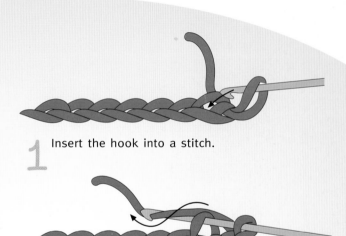

1 Insert the hook into a stitch.

2 Wrap the yarn around the hook. This is called a yarn over.

3 Grab the yarn with the hook and draw it through the stitch.

Getting Started

So now you have your hook and yarn. What do you do with them?

HOW TO HOLD YOUR HOOK

Although you may fiddle with your grip as you get more comfortable crocheting, there are basically two ways you can hold your hook—like a knife or like a pencil. See which one you like better.

Like a knife

Like a pencil

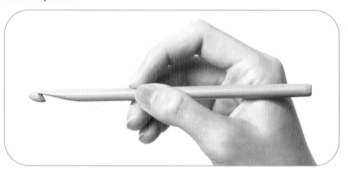

START WITH A SLIP KNOT

The first thing you need to do is secure your yarn to your hook so you can start crocheting. You do this with a **slip knot.**

1 Hold the long end of the yarn in one hand, about 8 inches from the end. With your other hand, loop the end of the yarn behind the yarn you're holding.

2 Pull some of the long end of the yarn through the loop and grab it with your hook.

3 Pull up your hook while holding the yarn below it. Tug on each strand of yarn to tighten the loop on your hook. Don't make the loop too tight—it should be snug, but loose enough to slide freely along the shaft.

The Stitches

Now that the yarn is on your hook, you're ready to go! Here's how to make the basic crochet stitches.

CHAIN STITCH

The basis of all of crochet is the **chain stitch** (abbreviated as **ch**) and it's pretty simple: you draw one loop of yarn through another. (Always start with a slip knot on your hook first!)

1 Wrap the yarn around your hook from back to front to back again. This is also called making a **yarn over**. Whenever you see an instruction to do a yarn over, that's what you do.

2 Grab the yarn with your hook, and draw it through the loop already on your hook.

3 You've made one chain stitch. Repeat steps 1 and 2 to make more chain stitches.

a chain is a chain is a...

It may seem a bit confusing that the word "chain" is used to refer to a couple different things. So let's take a minute to talk about these terms. A **chain stitch** is the most basic crochet stitch, and is the template on which all the other stitches are built.

When chain stitches are worked together in a row, this is called a **foundation chain.** When you start a project that's crocheted in rows, you will start with a foundation chain. When you start a project worked in rounds, you will work the first round into one chain stitch or into a small circle made up of a row of chain stitches attached to itself end to end.

Chain stitches are used in some patterns to create space between stitches for a lacy, open look. Chain stitches can also be used in the middle of the row to create a buttonhole.

check out your chain

After you've made several chain stitches, they'll form a **chain.** The front of a chain looks like a braid made up of v's. The back of a chain looks kind of like a spine, with a bumpy ridge down the middle. Your chain should be pretty loose so that you can easily insert your hook into it later. If your chain is too tight, it will be very difficult to work with, and the bottom edge of your project will not be smooth. Practice making chains until you're comfortable with the steps and the chains come out even and loose.

Front of the chain

Back of the chain

SLIP STITCH

Beyond the chain, the **slip stitch** (abbreviated as **sl st**) is the simplest crochet stitch. You won't use it to create a whole project, but it comes in handy, as you'll see!

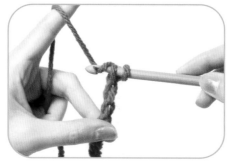

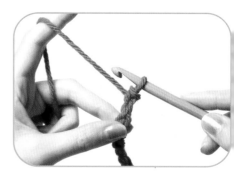

1 Insert your hook in a stitch (your pattern will tell you which one).

2 Yarn over. Then pull the yarn through both the stitch and the loop on your hook.

3 Now you have one loop on your hook, and you've completed one slip stitch. Repeat steps 1 and 2 to make your next stitch.

SINGLE CROCHET

The chain stitch may be the foundation of crochet, but the **single crochet** stitch (abbreviated as **sc**) is the basis for all the other stitches.

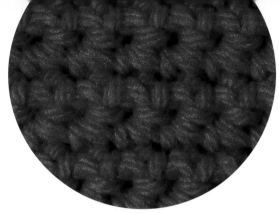

This is what several rows of single crochet stitches look like.

1 Insert your hook in the next stitch.

2 Yarn over.

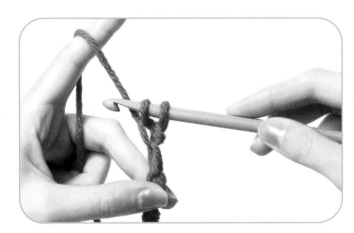

3 Grab the yarn that's over the hook and pull it through only the stitch (this is referred to as **pulling up a loop**). Now you have two loops on your hook.

4 Yarn over and pull the yarn through *both* of the loops on your hook. Now you have one loop on your hook, and you've just completed a single crochet stitch! Repeat steps 1–4 to make your next stitch.

HALF DOUBLE CROCHET

The rest of the crochet stitches are a variation of the single crochet stitch. Here's how to make a **half double crochet** (abbreviated as **hdc**).

1 Start with a yarn over. Then insert your hook in the next stitch.

2 Yarn over and pull up a loop. You now have three loops on your hook.

3 Yarn over and pull the yarn through all three loops on your hook. Now you have one loop on your hook, and you've completed one half double crochet stitch. Repeat steps 1–3 to make your next stitch.

tip Have fun experimenting with stitches. Check out a stitch dictionary—an entire book or website filled with fun stitches and stitch combinations. The possibilities are endless!

DOUBLE CROCHET

Have you noticed that the stitches keep getting taller as we go? Here's how to make a **double crochet** (abbreviated as **dc**).

1 Start with a yarn over. Then insert your hook in the next stitch.

2 Yarn over and pull up a loop. You now have three loops on your hook.

3 Yarn over and pull the yarn through the first two loops on your hook. Two loops remain on your hook.

4 Yarn over and pull the yarn through the remaining two loops on your hook. Now you have one loop on your hook, and you've completed one double crochet stitch. Repeat steps 1–4 to make your next stitch.

TREBLE CROCHET

Also referred to as **triple crochet** (and abbreviated as **tr**), this is a really tall stitch. Things get wild as we yarn over twice at the beginning of the stitch.

1 **Yarn over twice.** This means you wrap the yarn *twice* around the hook. Then insert your hook in the next stitch.

2 Yarn over and pull up a loop. You now have four loops on your hook.

3 Yarn over and pull the yarn through the first two loops on your hook. Now you have three loops on your hook.

4 Yarn over and pull the yarn through the first two loops on your hook. Two loops remain on your hook.

5 Yarn over and pull the yarn through the remaining two loops on your hook. Now you have one loop on your hook, and you've completed a treble crochet stitch. Repeat steps 1–5 to make your next stitch.

Crocheting in Rows

Projects such as scarves, belts, and sweaters are crocheted by working stitches in rows—one on top of another. When you finish one row, you turn the piece—really, you just flip it around—so the opposite side is facing you. Then you make another row on top of the one you just finished.

TURNING CHAINS

Crochet stitches are tall, so when you start a new row of stitches, you need to make one or more chain stitches, called **turning chains,** to gain the height needed to meet the top of the stitches you'll be making. Turning chains make the edges of your work neat and allow the piece to lay flat.

Depending on the pattern, turning chains are sometimes counted as a full stitch (this is common with the taller stitches), and sometimes they aren't. Each pattern will tell you whether the turning chain counts as a stitch or not.

You can make a turning chain at the end of a row, as shown here, or you can turn the work and make the chain at the beginning of the next row. The pattern will tell you where to work the turning chain.

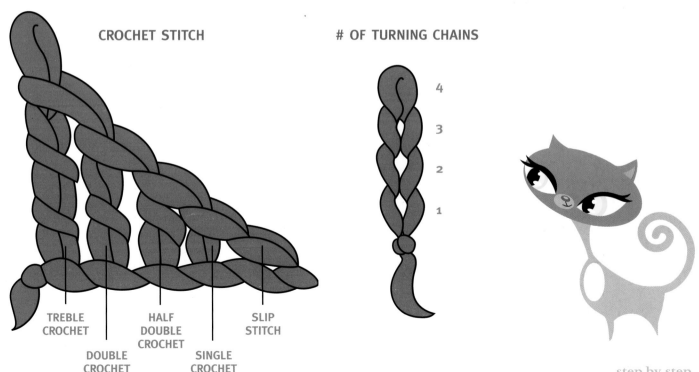

CROCHET STITCH

 # OF TURNING CHAINS

4

3

2

1

TREBLE CROCHET

DOUBLE CROCHET

HALF DOUBLE CROCHET

SINGLE CROCHET

SLIP STITCH

WHERE DOES YOUR HOOK GO?

To make stitches into the row below, you just insert your hook into a stitch. Take a look at the top of a row of stitches and you'll see that the top of a stitch looks like the front of a chain stitch, composed of a v. In most cases, you should insert your hook under both loops of the v. Sometimes, though, a pattern will instruct you to crochet into only one of the two loops of a stitch— the front loop or the back loop. Tilt your work again so you can see the tops of the stitches: the loop of the v that is closest to you is referred to as the **front loop** and the loop of the v that is farthest from you is referred to as the **back loop.**

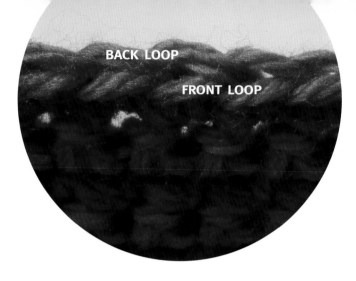

BACK LOOP

FRONT LOOP

To work into a stitch in the row below, insert your hook under both loops of the stitch.

To work into the **front loop only,** insert your hook into the loop closest to you, and work your stitches as usual.

To work into the **back loop only,** insert your hook into the loop farthest from you, and work your stitches as usual.

COUNTING STITCHES

You should count your stitches every few rows to make sure you have the correct number, especially when you're first learning how to crochet. It's easy to miss a stitch or to accidentally work more stitches than required.

Look at your stitches from above and you'll see the familiar braid. To count your stitches, you just count the v's in the braid.

To count the stitches several rows down, you count the "posts" of the stitches. (Remember to check your pattern to see if you should count the turning chain as a stitch.)

Attaching New Yarn

Unless you're making something small, you'll have to use more than one skein of yarn to complete a crochet project. So what happens when one skein runs out? You just start crocheting with another, of course! Use the same technique to change to yarn of a different color if you're making stripes. (In these photographs, the new yarn is shown in a different color to make the steps easier to see.)

AT THE BEGINNING OF A ROW

1 Leave a tail of the old yarn dangling. Attach the new yarn to your hook with a slip knot. Then insert your hook in the first stitch of the row.

2 Yarn over with the new yarn and pull up a loop. You now have two loops on your hook.

3 Yarn over and pull the yarn through the two loops on your hook. You've attached the new yarn. You'll then work the first stitch of the row with the new yarn in the same stitch where you just attached the yarn.

IN THE MIDDLE OF A ROW

1 With the old yarn, work the next stitch only up to the point where you have just one more step to do to complete it. Grab the new yarn with your hook.

2 Pull the new yarn through both loops on your hook to complete the stitch. You've attached the new yarn.

3 Complete the row as usual, following the pattern directions.

Finishing Off

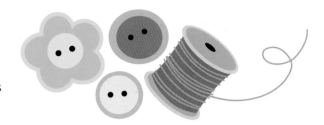

What do you do when you're all done crocheting? That's easy. You fasten off the yarn so your stitches won't unravel, and you weave in the yarn ends.

FASTENING OFF

When you have finished crocheting, you'll need to secure the yarn end. This is called **fastening off.** To do this, first cut the yarn, leaving a 6-inch tail.

1 Remove your hook from the final stitch, pulling up the loop a little so it doesn't unravel. Pull the yarn tail through the loop.

2 Tug the yarn tail to tighten the knot.

WEAVING IN YARN ENDS

When a crochet project is done, you'll have "tails" of yarn hanging off the project where you finished one ball of yarn and began another one. Use a yarn needle to weave the yarn tails into your piece, hiding them inside the loops of the stitches. This is called **weaving in ends.**

Use a yarn needle to weave one yarn tail at a time into the crochet stitches on the side of your work that won't show (that's called the **wrong side**). It's a good idea to change direction frequently, in a zigzag or wavy pattern, so the tails will stay put.

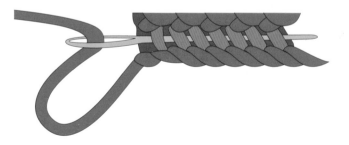

Checking Your Gauge

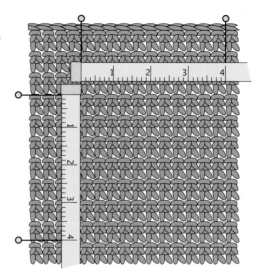

Gauge is the number of stitches and rows that fit in a given area of a piece of crochet. Most crochet patterns specify the gauge you need so that your work will end up with the same measurements as those given in the pattern. This makes sense, right? If the pattern calls for you to have a certain number of stitches in, say, 4 inches and you have more than that, then your work will end up too narrow. If you have fewer stitches in 4 inches, then your work will end up too wide. Take a second and think on that until it makes perfect sense.

You should always make a **gauge swatch** before you begin a project. A swatch is a piece of crochet, usually about 5 inches square, worked with the same yarn, the same size crochet hook, and the same stitches specified in the pattern. By making a swatch before you begin your project, you can make sure your work produces the same number of stitches and rows called for in the pattern. If you have too many stitches, you should try again using a larger hook. If you have too few stitches, you should try again using a smaller hook.

To make a gauge swatch, start with a chain about 5 inches long. Then work rows in the stitches called for in your pattern until your piece is about 5 inches high. Fasten off. To measure, lay a ruler or tape measure horizontally across a row. Count how many stitches fit in 4 inches in the middle of the swatch. (You don't want to count along the edges—that's why you crochet a 5-inch square in order to measure a 4-inch area.) Next, lay the ruler across the center of the swatch vertically and count how many rows fit in 4 inches.

oops!

Whether you're first learning to crochet or you're a seasoned pro, you may find that—even with careful counting—you've made a mistake somewhere and have the wrong number of stitches in a row. Before you rip out your work to the point where you made the mistake, take a good look at it so you can see what you did wrong.

If you accidentally added or skipped one stitch several rows back, you can simply increase or decrease by one stitch in your current row to correct it. (You'll learn how in the next chapter.) If, however, you're several stitches off, you may just want to rip back to the row containing the error and rework it with the correct number of stitches. To rip back, just remove the hook from your work and gently tug on the yarn to unravel the stitches.

Chunky Scarf

Pattern by Kim Werker

SKILLS Chain, half double crochet, joining new yarn, weaving in ends

Practice your swank new crochet skills and make yourself a fun scarf while you're at it! When you're finished, you'll be an expert at working rows of half double crochet, changing colors (adding new balls of yarn), and weaving in ends.

FINISHED MEASUREMENTS

6 feet x 6 inches

MATERIALS

* Lion Brand Wool-Ease Chunky yarn (80% acrylic, 20% wool; 153 yds/140 m per 5 oz/140 g): 1 skein each in Orchid [Color A], Pumpkin [Color B], and Fisherman [Color C]
* 10 mm (size P) hook
* Yarn needle

> **tip**
> If you want to make a skinnier scarf, begin with fewer than 13 chains. If you want to make a wider scarf, make more chains.

6'

6"

GAUGE

7½ stitches/7 rows = 4 inches in half double crochet [Note: Gauge is not important for a scarf.]

PATTERN

* With Color A, chain 13.
* Row 1: Work 1 half double crochet into the third chain from your hook. Work 1 half double crochet into each of the remaining chains, to end up with 11 stitches in total. Chain 2, then turn your work so the turning chain you just made is now on the right if you're right-handed. It should be on the left if you're left-handed.
* Row 2: Half double crochet into each stitch across the row. The turning chain does not count as a stitch in this pattern, so don't skip the first stitch, and make sure to count your stitches at the end of the row—you should have 11 in total. Chain 2, turn.
* Rows 3–31: Half double crochet into each stitch across. Chain 2, turn.
* Row 32: Half double crochet into each stitch until you have just 1 more stitch to make. Yarn over, insert your hook into the last stitch and pull up a loop. There are now 3 loops on your hook, and your stitch is one step away from being completed. Leaving a tail 6 inches long, cut the Color A yarn. Drop Color A and pick up Color C. Leave a 6-inch tail, and complete the final stitch with Color C yarn. Chain 2, turn.
* Row 33: Half double crochet into each stitch across, changing back to Color A in the final stitch. Chain 2, turn.
* Rows 34–38: Half double crochet into each stitch across, changing to Color C at the end of Row 38. Chain 2, turn.
* Row 39: Half double crochet into each stitch across, changing to Color A in the final stitch. Chain 2, turn.

more

* Rows 40–42: Half double crochet into each stitch across, changing to Color C at the end of Row 42. Chain 2, turn.

* Rows 43–44: Half double crochet into each stitch across, changing to Color A at the end of Row 44. Chain 2, turn.

* Rows 45–46: Half double crochet into each stitch across, changing to Color C at the end of Row 46. Chain 2, turn.

* Rows 47–61: Half double crochet into each stitch across, changing to Color B at the end of Row 61. Chain 2, turn.

* Rows 62–63: Half double crochet into each stitch across, changing to Color C at the end of Row 63. Chain 2, turn.

* Rows 64–65: Half double crochet into each stitch across, changing to Color B at the end of Row 65. Chain 2, turn.

* Rows 66–68: Half double crochet into each stitch across, changing to Color C at the end of Row 68. Chain 2, turn.

* Row 69: Half double crochet into each stitch across, changing to Color B in the final stitch. Chain 2, turn.

* Rows 70–74: Half double crochet into each stitch across, changing to Color C at the end of Row 74. Chain 2, turn.

* Row 75: Half double crochet into each stitch across, changing to Color B in the final stitch. Chain 2, turn.

* Rows 76–107: Half double crochet into each stitch across. Cut yarn, leaving a 6-inch tail, and fasten off.

FINISHING

Weave in the yarn ends. Come on, it's not that bad! If it's too tedious, rent a movie with some friends. By the time the movie's over you'll have all those ends woven in, and a fab new scarf to show off!

watching while you work

Once you've gotten the hang of working simple stitches in rows, you won't need to concentrate so hard on what your hands are doing. It can be relaxing and enjoyable to crochet while watching TV, on your own or with friends. Here are some fun movies you can rent— some celebrate creativity and crafting with others, and some are just about having a good time with friends. When you choose a movie to watch, keep in mind that your crochet can be affected by your emotional state—if you watch a horror movie or a tense drama, you might make tighter stitches than usual.

* *The Breakfast Club* (1985)
* *How to Make an American Quilt* (1995)
* *Clueless* (1995)
* *Divine Secrets of the Ya-Ya Sisterhood* (2002)
* *Mean Girls* (2004)
* *The Sisterhood of the Traveling Pants* (2005)

crochet for good

*C*rocheting for others—especially for people in need—is a great way to share your talents and do some good at the same time.

THE CHARITIES There are many charities that accept donated crocheted items. For a start, you can check out the Crochet Guild of America's list of charities (see page 94). You can also find organizations in your area that accept handmade goods. Try asking at your local hospital, fire department, shelters, religious organizations, and other groups you think might benefit from what you can make. Ask your local yarn shop if they participate in a charitable program.

THE PROJECTS Organizations distribute caps to premature babies, soft hats to hospital patients, afghans to homebound elders, hats and scarves to the less fortunate, and so much more. Just about any item that you enjoy making will certainly be appreciated by someone less fortunate.

THE CROCHETERS You can crochet at home and bring the items you plan to donate to the charity, but you can also make crocheting for charity a group project, either with your best buds or with an after-school club. With a group of friends, you can each work on individual squares and then put them together to make one large item, such as an afghan. You could organize a group at your school to crochet items to donate as a community service project.

3

around she goes

Ready for this? If you crochet around
and around, adding more stitches
each time, you'll create…a circle!
Use these techniques to make a
cottony-soft, face-friendly washcloth.

Increasing

There's more to crochet than just making rectangles! By adding stitches to make your rows longer you can shape your work in lots of ways. This is called **increasing**—you work two stitches in the same place, thus adding one stitch to your total number of stitches. Many patterns use this to create pretty and unusual textures. Here's how to increase by one stitch:

1 Insert your hook in the same stitch you just worked into.

2 Complete the stitch as usual. You've now made two stitches in the same stitch.

Take a close look at the row you've just completed and you can see where you worked two stitches in the same place.

shape it up

You can use carefully placed increases to make all sorts of shapes. By placing an increase at the beginning and end of each row, you can make a triangle or a trapezoid. By placing increases at regular intervals in crocheting in the round, you can make a circle (see page 40). If you place many increases in every stitch of a rectangle, the fabric will turn in and out and you'll end up with a funky ruffle. Experiment to see what you can come up with!

Working in the Round

When you want to make rounded shapes instead of rectangles, you work in rounds rather than in rows, which is called, appropriately enough, **working in the round.** You don't turn your work after each round as you do with rows—you just keep going around and around. Increasing is an important part of crocheting in the round. You start in the very center of the circle and increase regularly so your work lays nice and flat. Here's how to work in the round:

1 To work in the round, start out with a chain— the number of chain stitches you make will be specified in the pattern you're following. In this example, it's a chain of six.

tip

You can also form a ring by working several stitches into the same foundation chain stitch. You'll try this out in the Fresh-Face Washcloth pattern on page 42.

2 To join the chain, make a slip stitch in the very first chain to form a ring.

3 To make your first round, insert your hook into the center of the ring—not into an individual chain stitch. You are going to work each of the next stitches around the ring itself.

5 To do a second round, start with a turning chain (usually you don't turn your work when you work in the round, but you still call it a turning chain), and crochet as usual.

4 When you have gone all the way around, join the last stitch to the first with a slip stitch. You have now completed one round.

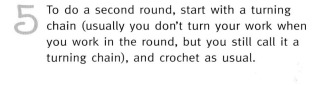

using stitch markers

When you work in the round it's easy to lose track of where one round ends and another begins, so it's a good idea to mark the start of each round with a **stitch marker,** which you'll move "up" as your work progresses. Just put the stitch marker in the first stitch of the first round. When you are ready to work the next round, take out the marker and work the first stitch in the new round. Then immediately place the marker in the stitch you just made.

Fresh-Face Washcloth

Pattern by Kim Werker

SKILLS Chain, slip stitch, double crochet, increasing, working in the round, weaving in ends

Working in the round is really easy. Practice by making this super-simple cotton washcloth. When you're done you'll be a pro, and you'll have something to make you feel special every time you wash your face!

FINISHED MEASUREMENT

About 7½ inches in diameter

7½"

MATERIALS

* 1 ball Bernat Cotton Tots yarn (100% cotton; 200 yds/182 m per 4 oz/113 g) in Blue Berry
* 5.5 mm (size I) hook
* Yarn needle

PATTERN

This washcloth is made of double crochet stitches worked in the round. You make only two turning chains (instead of the three usually made for double crochet), and the turning chain does not count as a stitch. This helps to hide the join in each round and makes a prettier circle.

* Chain 3.

* Round 1: Work 8 double crochets into the first chain. Because of the slip knot, the first chain will grow in size to accommodate all of the stitches. Slip stitch in the first double crochet to join the round—8 double crochets total.

* Round 2: Chain 2. Increase once in each stitch around by working 2 double crochets in each stitch, including the one you just slip stitched in. Slip stitch in the first double crochet to join the round—16 double crochets total.

* Round 3: Chain 2. Double crochet in the first stitch (this is the same stitch you just slip stitched in). Work 2 double crochets in the next stitch (1 increase made). *Double crochet in the next stitch, work 2 double crochets in the next stitch.* Repeat from * to * all the way around. Slip stitch in the first double crochet to join the round—24 double crochets total.

* Round 4: Chain 2. Double crochet in each of the first 2 stitches, then work 2 double crochets in the next stitch. *Double crochet in each of the next 2 stitches, work 2 double crochets in the next stitch.* Repeat from * to * around. Slip stitch in the first double crochet to join the round—32 double crochets total.

* Round 5: Chain 2. Double crochet in each of the first 3 stitches, then work 2 double crochets in the next stitch. *Double crochet in each of the next 3 stitches, work 2 double crochets in the next stitch.* Repeat from * to * around. Slip stitch in the first double crochet to join the round—40 double crochets total.

* Round 6: Chain 2. Double crochet in each of the first 4 stitches, then work 2 double crochets in the next stitch. *Double crochet in each of the next 4 stitches, work 2 double crochets in the next stitch.* Repeat from * to * around. Slip stitch in the first double crochet to join the round—48 double crochets total.

more

* Round 7: Chain 2. Double crochet in each of the first 5 stitches, then work 2 double crochets in the next stitch. *Double crochet in each of the next 5 stitches, work 2 double crochets in the next stitch.* Repeat from * to * around. Slip stitch in the first double crochet to join the round—56 double crochets total.

* Round 8: Chain 2. Double crochet in each of the first 6 stitches, then work 2 double crochets in the next stitch. *Double crochet in each of the next 6 stitches, work 2 double crochets in the next stitch.* Repeat from * to * around. Slip stitch in the first double crochet to join the round—64 double crochets total.

Now make a little loop to hang your washcloth.

* Chain 10, make a slip stitch in the stitch at the bottom of the chain. Fasten off and weave in the yarn ends.

* If your washcloth doesn't lie perfectly flat, you can block it (see below).

Make your washcloth more fun by adding an edging! (See page 48 for more on edgings.) The simplest edging to make is to work a round of single crochet in a different color. Instead of fastening off at the end of the pattern, change to a new color and work one more round (or two) in single crochet, continuing to increase regularly so the washcloth lays flat.

blocking

Crocheted fabric has a tendency to curl or twist, and some pieces may not be perfectly square or round when completed. To make your project look neat when you're finished (especially if it's made of natural fibers), you can block it.

Lay your project out on a firm, flat, cushioned surface—on your bed, on a clean carpet, or on several folded towels. Pin it into the shape you want, using rust-proof pins. Lightly spray it evenly with water. Allow the piece to air dry (overnight, if necessary). When you take out the pins, your project will retain the shape.

Pin the crocheted piece to a cushioned surface such as a towel and then lightly spray it evenly with water.

crochet with friends

Crocheting is a great way to relax and enjoy some alone time, but it can also be fun to crochet with your friends. Not only will you have quality time with one another, but you can share projects and learn cool tips, too.

HOST A LEARN-TO-CROCHET PARTY Invite a bunch of friends over and buy some yarn and hooks so you can teach them the basics. Make yummy snacks, grab throw pillows so everyone's comfy sitting on the floor, and have a fabulous crochet night!

If you know other great crocheters— your grandmother, your best friend's aunt—invite them over to teach you and your friends how to crochet.

START A CROCHET CLUB Set up a time to meet weekly or monthly—as often as you want. Check with your school to see if you can meet after classes at the end of the day. You can organize crochet classes, have tips-'n'-tricks presentations so members can show off their skills, and admire everyone's great work!

TEACH OTHERS Once you all know how to crochet, gather your buds and volunteer together at an elementary school or after-school program for younger kids, so you can teach them how to crochet, too!

less is more

Ready for more? Learn how to decrease—when you work fewer stitches in each row or round—and you can go beyond just making circles and rectangles. Make a big triangle and you'll have a hip-looking head scarf!

Decreasing

Sometimes you want fewer stitches in your row or round because you want your work to get smaller. So to do that you need to **decrease,** and there are two common ways to do that. You can decrease within a row by working two or more stitches together; this will produce a gradual, slanting decrease. Or you can decrease by leaving stitches at the beginning or end of a row unworked. This will produce a dramatic decrease with sharp angles.

WORKING STITCHES TOGETHER

1 Work the next stitch only up to the point where you have two loops remaining on your hook (in other words, work the stitch until you only have to do one more step to complete it).

2 Insert your hook in the next stitch, and again work the stitch only up to the point at which you have to do one more step to complete it. Because you already had two loops on your hook, you now have three loops.

3 Yarn over and pull the yarn through all three loops. You have just worked two stitches together. Look closely, and you will see that there is only one v at the top of the two stitches you worked together.

LEAVING STITCHES UNWORKED

At the beginning of a row

At the beginning of a row, work a slip stitch in each stitch you want to appear to be unworked. After "skipping" those stitches, make a chain to create the height you need to start making the next stitches, and continue across the row.

At the end of a row

At the end of a row, simply stop working and just make a turning chain. Turn your work, leaving the rest of the stitches unworked.

Cool Edges

One of the features that makes crochet so versatile is that you can pretty much stick your hook anywhere. Sure, you usually work into stitches from previous rows or rounds. But you can also make a border around an entire piece by working into the fabric sideways, inserting your hook into the spaces between rows.

BASIC EDGING

The simplest edging you can do is to work a row (or more) of slip stitch or single crochet around your piece. You can do this whether your piece is round or rectangular.

On a round Join the new yarn where you fastened off the last round. Chain 1, then work a single crochet in the same stitch you pulled the yarn through.

* Edging round: Work 1 single crochet in each stitch around, making the same number of increases (working 2 single crochets in the same stitch) as you did in the last round of the piece. For example, if you wanted to add an edging to the Fresh-Face Washcloth on page 42, you would make 8 increases in the edging round, just like you made 8 increases in each round of the washcloth.

* Slip stitch in the first edge stitch to join the round. You can fasten off, or chain 1 and continue to work a second round of single crochet for a wider edging.

Around a rectangle Starting in the top right corner, join the new yarn. Chain 1 and work 1 single crochet in the same stitch you pulled the yarn through.

* Edging row: Work 1 single crochet in each stitch across the top of the piece until only 1 stitch remains to be worked. Work 3 single crochets into the final stitch for the corner (this turns your work around the corner).

* Don't flip your work around as you would if you were going to work a new row, but rotate it 90 degrees clockwise so you can keep crocheting along the next side. Work 1 single crochet into each space between the rows. Work 3 stitches into the final space for the corner. Continue working around the shape, until you get back to the beginning of the border.

* Slip stitch in the first edge stitch to join the border. You can fasten off, or chain 1 and continue to work a second row of single crochet for a wider border.

PICOT EDGING

Picots are easy to make. You just make a short chain and slip stitch into the bottom of it to make a little ball of yarn. You need an odd number of stitches to work a symmetrical picot edging. Join the new yarn and make a single crochet in the first stitch.

* Picot row: *Chain 3, and make a slip stitch in the first chain (the one farthest from your hook). Skip 1 stitch, and make a single crochet in the next stitch.* Repeat from * to *, working all around the item. Fasten off.

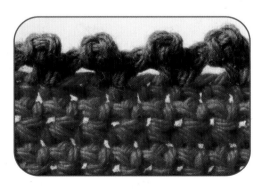

Fringe

Adding fringe is a great way to finish off the end of a belt or scarf, or any other rectangular or triangular project. You start by cutting lengths of yarn that are twice as long as you want the fringe to be, then you attach them to your project. So easy! You can make fringe from a single strand of yarn, or from many strands. You choose.

SINGLE-STRAND FRINGE

Start by cutting a piece of yarn that is twice as long as you want the fringe to be.

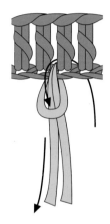

1 Fold the strand in half. Use a crochet hook to pull the strand through the crocheted piece.

2 Now use the hook to grab the two yarn ends and pull them through the loop. Tug the ends to tighten.

MANY-STRAND FRINGE

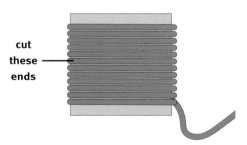

cut these ends

1 Wrap yarn around a square piece of cardboard or a CD jewel case. The more wraps you make the thicker the tassel will be. Cut the yarn along one edge of the cardboard or jewel case.

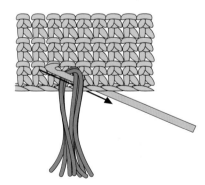

2 Keep the strands folded in half. Using a large crochet hook (it needs to be pretty big, so it can grab all the strands at once), pull the fold through the crocheted piece.

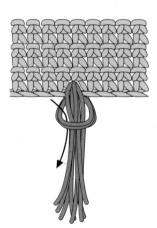

3 Now draw all the loose ends through the loop of the fold and tug on them to tighten. Trim the ends so they're even.

TRY IT! Hipster Head Scarf

Pattern by Kim Werker

SKILLS Chain, slip stitch, single crochet, decreasing, weaving in ends

Make this fun head scarf to get the hang of decreasing! You start at the wide end of the triangle and decrease in every single row down to the point. Add a pretty picot edging around all three sides for extra flair.

FINISHED MEASUREMENTS

20½ inches wide x 9 inches high with the edging, plus ties (approximately 13 inches each)

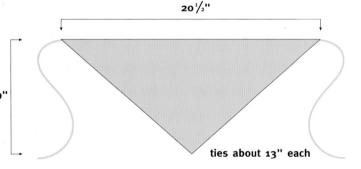

20½"

9"

ties about 13" each

MATERIALS

* 1 ball Crystal Palace Yarns Mikado Ribbon yarn (50% cotton, 50% viscose; 112 yds per 50 g) in Tulips
* 5.5 mm (size I) hook
* Yarn needle

PATTERN

* Chain 66.
* Row 1: Single crochet in the second chain from your hook, and in each chain across. Chain 1, turn—65 single crochets total.

* Row 2: Work the first 2 single crochets together (1 decrease made). Single crochet in each stitch until 2 stitches remain. Work the last 2 single crochets together (another decrease made)—63 single crochets total.
* Rows 3–32: Repeat Row 2, continuing to decrease twice in each row (once at the beginning and once at the end) until 3 stitches remain. Fasten off.

Picot border and ties

The head scarf is shaped like a triangle. Work a picot border around the two short sides first, then make the ties at the same time you make the border on the long side.

* Lay the triangle down right side up, with the longest side closest to you. Attach yarn to the bottom-right corner, and work the picot edging around the two short sides as follows (working into the spaces between the rows):
* Single crochet in the side of the first stitch.
* *Chain 3, slip stitch in the first chain (the one farthest from your hook). Skip 1 space, single crochet in the next space.* Repeat from * to *, working the picot edging around the point of the triangle and down the second short side. Fasten off.

Now make the ties.

* Using new yarn, chain 45 (this will be the first tie). Slip stitch in the first stitch of the long side of the triangle (the foundation chain).
* You'll now make the picot edging. Single crochet in the same stitch where you just worked a slip stitch. *Chain 3, slip stitch in the first chain (the one farthest from your hook). Skip 1 stitch, single crochet in the next stitch.* Repeat from * to * until you've worked into the last stitch in the triangle.
* Chain 45 (for the second tie). Fasten off and weave in the yarn ends.

5

the patterns!

Rock on with crochet! This chapter includes twelve fabulous patterns full of texture and color—from cool containers for all your girly goods, to wrist cuffs you can share with your friends, to a sparkly skirt sized just for you.

Beauty Bin and Ring Cave

Pattern by Melissa Hills

SKILLS Chain, single crochet, weaving in ends, seaming

Every cool girl needs a place to keep her small stuff! These cute containers are easy to crochet and take no time at all. Gauge isn't important in this project—just make sure your stitches are tight so the pieces will stand up once you sew them together.

FINISHED MEASUREMENTS

Bin: 3 inches wide x 3 inches high x 3 inches deep
Cave: 2¾ inches wide x 1½ inches high x 1¾ inches deep

bottom
3¼" x 3¼"

side
3½" x 3½"

bin

A — A

7"

B — B

cave

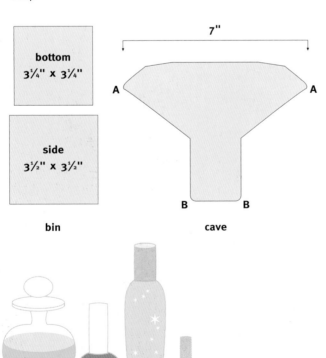

MATERIALS

* 1 ball Bernat Cotton Tots yarn (100% cotton; 200 yds/183 m per 4oz/113 g) in Strawberry
* 3.75 mm (size F) crochet hook, or size needed to produce tight stitches
* 1 package 10 mm pailettes (available at craft stores)
* Yarn needle
* Straight pins
* Sewing needle and thread to match yarn

GAUGE

About 8 stitches/9 rows = 2 inches
[Note: Gauge is not important here as long as your stitches are tight enough to give the container a little structure once it's assembled—which is why you use a smaller hook than the yarn label recommends.]

BEAUTY BIN

Sides (make 4)
* Chain 16.
* Row 1: Single crochet in the second chain from your hook and in each chain across—15 single crochets total. Turn.
* Row 2: Chain 1. Single crochet in each stitch across. Turn.
* Rows 3–14: Repeat Row 2.
* Fasten off and weave in the yarn ends.

Bottom
* Chain 14.
* Row 1: Single crochet in the second chain from your hook and in each chain across—13 single crochets total. Turn.
* Row 2: Chain 1. Single crochet in each stitch. Turn.
* Rows 3–14: Repeat Row 2.
* Fasten off and weave in the yarn ends.

more

FINISHING

The beauty bin is sewn together with the seams on the outside.

1. Place two of the sides together with the wrong sides facing each other. Using yarn and a yarn needle, whip stitch (see page 57) along the long edge. Repeat with the other side pieces until you have all four pieces sewn together.

2. Whip stitch the bottom to the sides.

3. Using a sewing needle and thread, sew one pailette to each side of the container.

RING CAVE

* Chain 20.

* Row 1: Single crochet in 3rd chain from hook (the 2 chains you skip count as your first single crochet) and in each chain across—19 single crochets total. Chain 1 (this chain counts as your first single crochet in each row), turn.

* Row 2: Start decreases as follows: Skip the first 2 stitches, single crochet in each of next 15 stitches, skip 1 stitch and single crochet in the top of the turning chain—17 single crochets total. Chain 1, turn.

* Row 3: Skip the first 2 stitches, single crochet in each of next 13 stitches, skip 1 stitch and single crochet in the top of the turning chain—15 single crochets total. Chain 1, turn.

* Row 4: Skip the first 2 stitches, single crochet in each of next 11 stitches, skip 1 stitch and single crochet in the top of the turning chain—13 single crochets total. Chain 1, turn.

* Row 5: Skip the first 2 stitches, single crochet in each of next 9 stitches, skip 1 stitch and single crochet in the top of the turning chain—11 single crochets total. Chain 1, turn.

* Row 6: Skip the first 2 stitches, single crochet in each of next 7 stitches, skip 1 stitch and single crochet in the top of the turning chain—9 single crochets total. Chain 1, turn.

* Row 7: Skip the first 2 stitches, single crochet in each of next 5 stitches, skip 1 stitch and single crochet in the top of the turning chain—7 single crochets total. Chain 1, turn.

* Rows 8–14: Single crochet in each stitch across. Chain 1, turn.

* Row 15: Single crochet in each stitch across. Fasten off and weave in the yarn ends.

FINISHING

1. Bring corner A to corner B on each side and pin along these edges, forming a "cave."

2. With yarn and a yarn needle, whip stitch along these edges.

3. Using a sewing needle and thread, sew one pailette to the inside of the ring cave so that it hangs down into the opening.

front and back

When you crochet something that has an inside and an outside, such as a garment, or a bag or box where one side shows and the other side doesn't, the outside is referred to as the **right side,** and the inside is referred to as the **wrong side.** When you crochet in rows, each side of the fabric looks the same, since you turn your work after each row. In this case, you can arbitrarily pick which side is the right side. If you're crocheting in the round without turning your work, it's usually assumed that the side of the work that's facing you as you crochet is the right side, but you can always choose to make it the wrong side if you want. Just remember that the wrong side is the side you'll weave your yarn ends into, because it's the side that will be hidden from view.

stitching it all together

There are several ways you can assemble crocheted pieces—here we'll show you three of them. Usually you hold the two crocheted pieces with right sides together, so the seams will be hidden on the inside of the completed object. But sometimes a seam can be used for decoration; in that case, you place the wrong sides together to keep the seam on the outside of your finished project. Whichever way you choose to seam, use the same yarn that you used to make the project. (In these photos, we show a contrasting-color yarn so you can see how to make the stitches.)

WHIP STITCH SEAM Whip stitching is an easy way to sew two pieces together. It's such a pretty stitch, though, you may just want to make it on the outside of your work!

Insert the needle from front to back through the first stitch of both pieces and pull the yarn through, leaving a 6-inch tail. Bring the needle back around to the front, and insert it from front to back through the next stitch of both pieces. Pull the yarn through. Repeat.

SLIP STITCH SEAM You can also crochet your pieces together. Crocheted seams are very strong, but they can also be a bit bulky. If you used a chunky yarn to crochet with, you may want to use a matching thinner yarn to make your seam.

Attach your seaming yarn to the hook with a slip knot. Holding the pieces with right sides together, insert your hook in the first stitch of both pieces, and make a slip stitch. Continue along the edge, making slip stitches through both pieces.

SINGLE CROCHET SEAM The single crochet seam is bulky, and is often left on the outside of a finished piece because it adds a raised, decorative detail.

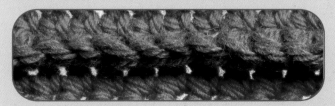

Attach the seaming yarn to the hook with a slip knot. Holding the pieces with wrong sides together (so the seam will show on the outside), insert your hook in the first stitch of both pieces, and make a single crochet stitch. Continue along the edge, making single crochet stitches through both pieces.

Bracelet Baglet

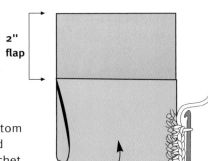

Pattern by Cecily Keim

SKILLS Chain, slip stitch, single crochet, half double crochet, weaving in ends, seaming

*g*otta run but don't want to carry a huge purse? Just toss your essentials into this fun little bag, slip it on your wrist, and you're off! These are so easy to make, you can whip one up for every outfit.

MEASUREMENTS

Unfinished: 4½ x 9 inches

Finished: 4½ x 3½ inches, without strap

MATERIALS

* 1 ball Crystal Palace Shimmer yarn (86% acrylic, 14% nylon; 90 yds per 50g) in Celery
* 5.0 mm (size H) hook
* 2 beaded bracelets, one to take apart for the fastener
* Sewing needle and thread to match yarn

GAUGE

4 stitches/4 rows = 4 inches

PATTERN

* Chain 21.
* Row 1: Single crochet in the second chain from your hook and in each chain across—20 single crochets total. Chain 1, turn.
* Row 2: Single crochet in the first stitch. *Slip stitch in the next stitch, half double crochet in the next stitch.* Repeat from * to * to the last stitch of the row. Single crochet in the last stitch. Chain 1, turn.
* Rows 3–36: Repeat Row 2.
* Row 37: Single crochet in each stitch across. Fasten off and weave in the yarn ends.

Strap

* Using new yarn and leaving a 6-inch tail, chain 16.
* Row 1: Single crochet in the second chain from your hook and in each chain across. Chain 1, turn.
* Row 2: Half double crochet in each stitch across. Chain 1, turn.
* Row 3: Single crochet in the first stitch and in each stitch across. Fasten off, leaving a 6-inch tail (the tail will be used later to attach the strap to the bag).

FINISHING

1. Fold the rectangle lengthwise, as shown, leaving a 2-inch flap that will fold over the top of the purse.

2. Join yarn at the bottom corner of one side and seam using single crochet (see page 57). Fasten off. Repeat for the other side.

1" **9"** **6"** **– fold** **strap** **4½"** **bag**

2" flap **fold**

3. Fold the strap over one of the bracelets and sew the short ends together using one of the yarn tails. Close the flap of the baglet and sew the strap to the top back of the baglet using the other yarn tail. Fasten off and weave in yarn ends.

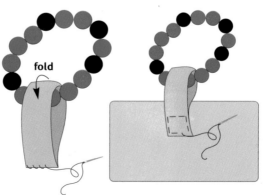

fold

4. To make a fastener, cut the string or elastic holding together the second beaded bracelet. Using sewing needle and thread, sew two of the beads to the front of the bag under the flap, about $\frac{1}{2}$ inch from the top and about 2 inches apart. The fabric of the flap is loose enough so that you can just pop the beads through the stitches to close the baglet. Or you could sew on buttons for the fastener rather than using beads from a second bracelet.

the patterns! 59

Beaded Bookmark

Pattern by Donna Hulka

SKILLS Chain, slip stitch, single crochet

This simple yet elegant bookmark is really easy to make. You crochet a long chain, slide a bead onto it, and then slip stitch back down the chain, ending up where you began. The most important part of this project is keeping your tension even. If you're a beginning crocheter, you may want to practice on a sample chain first.

FINISHED MEASUREMENT

About 12 inches long, not including bead and tassel

MATERIALS

* 7 yards of size 3 crochet thread or fingering weight yarn, such as J. & P. Coats Royale Fashion Crochet Size 3 Thread or Aunt Lydia's Fashion Crochet Size 3 Thread
* 3.50 mm (size E) crochet hook
* 1 round or oval bead, 12 mm to 20 mm in diameter
* 5-inch square of cardboard or CD jewel case (to make the tassel)
* 1 large crochet hook, 6.0–9.0 mm (size J, K, or N) (for attaching the tassel)

GAUGE

20 chain stitches = 4 inches
24 chain stitches with slip stitches = 4 inches
(After slip stitching in the chain stitches, the chain will become shorter.)
[Note: Gauge is not important here as long as your stitches are even.]

PATTERN

* Leaving a 6-inch tail, make a slip knot. Check the slip knot to make sure it is tight; this will make it easier for the bead to pass over it.
* Chain 82.
* Starting at the tail, slide the bead over the slip knot and onto the chain. Slide the bead close to the end where you are working, about 2 to 3 chain stitches from your hook.
* Now make a single crochet around the chain to secure the bead. To do this, don't insert your hook into a chain stitch but rather make a single crochet around the whole chain, near the bead. Make sure the stitch is snug, not loose.
* Without removing your hook, slide the single crochet stitch as close to the bead as possible. You'll probably need to adjust the bead a little bit so it is centered in the stitch.
* Now you'll slip stitch down the chain, working each stitch into the back loop (spine) of the chain (see page 30). (By working into the back loops, the bookmark will look the same on both sides and resemble a braid.) To make the first slip stitch, place your hook into the back loop of the next chain stitch closest to your single crochet. Continue to slip stitch down the chain until you have 4 chain stitches left.

Now make the loop for the tassel.

* Chain 3, skip the next 3 chain stitches, and slip stitch in the last chain stitch. Leaving a 6-inch tail, fasten off. You don't have to weave in the yarn ends—they will become part of the fringe.

1. Make the many-strand fringe on page 49.

2. Keeping the strands folded in half, use a large crochet hook to draw the fold through the hole at the end of the bookmark.

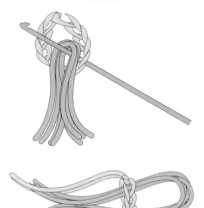

3. Now draw the loose ends of the strands (along with the two tail ends of the bookmark) through the loop made by the fold, and tighten. Trim the ends evenly.

beads

When choosing your bead, make sure the hole is large enough to slide over the crocheted chain. Note that glass beads up to about 14mm are fine, but larger ones tend to be too heavy to work well as a bookmark. Plastic and wooden beads are much lighter in weight, even in larger sizes.

Sushi Roll Pillow

Pattern by MK Carroll

SKILLS Chain, slip stitch, double crochet, increasing, seaming, working in the round, joining new yarn, making a buttonhole, weaving in ends

What will Mom say about sushi on the sofa? Yum! Add some flair to your living room or bedroom with this easy pillow. It's super-soft, cuddly, and über cool.

FINISHED MEASUREMENT
12-inch diameter

MATERIALS
* Lion Brand Microspun yarn (100% microfiber acrylic; 168 yds/154m per 2.5 oz/70g): 2 skeins in Lily White, 1 skein each in Ebony, Cherry Red, Lime, and Buttercup
* 4mm (size G) hook
* Stitch markers
* Yarn needle
* Sewing needle and thread to match yarn
* Five ³⁄₄-inch buttons
* 12-inch round pillow form or insert, or materials to make your own (see box on page 65)

GAUGE
4 stitches/4 rows = 1 inch in double crochet stitch worked in the round

PATTERN
The very center of the pillow (the sushi filling) is made of three wedges in different colors that are crocheted back and forth in rows. After these center wedges are completed and sewn together in a circle, the rest of the pillow is crocheted in the round, first with white (the rice) and then with black (the nori).

Front
Start with the center filling. Make one each with Cherry Red, Lime, and Buttercup.

* Chain 3.
* Row 1: Skip 2 chains, then double crochet three times into the last chain—3 stitches total. Turn.
* Row 2: Chain 2. Double crochet twice in each stitch across—6 stitches total. Turn.
* Row 3: Chain 2. Double crochet in the first stitch, double crochet twice in each of the next 4 stitches, then double crochet in the last stitch—10 stitches total. Turn.
* Row 4: Chain 2. Double crochet in the first 2 stitches, double crochet twice in each of the next 2 stitches, double crochet in the next 2 stitches, double crochet twice in each of the next 2 stitches, double crochet in the last 2 stitches—14 stitches total. Turn.
* Row 5: Chain 2. Double crochet in the next 3 stitches, double crochet twice in each of the next 3 stitches, double crochet in the next 2 stitches, double crochet twice in each of the next 3 stitches, double crochet in the last 3 stitches—20 stitches total. Turn.
* Row 6: Chain 2. Double crochet in the next 5 stitches, double crochet twice in each of the next 3 stitches, double crochet in the next 4 stitches, double crochet twice in each of the next 3 stitches, double crochet in the last 5 stitches—26 stitches total.

more ➤

* Cut the yarn, leaving a 6-inch tail, and fasten off.
* When all three wedges are complete, sew them together to form a disk. Place two of the wedges right sides together, and sew them together using a whip stitch. Then sew the third wedge to the other two so they form a circle.

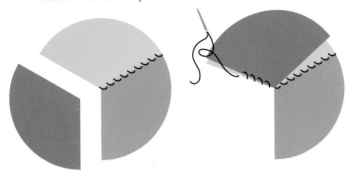

Now crochet the rice, working in the round.

* Round 1: With Lily White yarn, insert your hook into any of the outer stitches of the sushi filling, draw the yarn through, and chain 2. Double crochet in the same stitch and in each stitch all around the sushi filling—78 stitches total. Slip stitch in the first stitch to join the round.

* Round 2: Chain 2. Double crochet twice in the first stitch (1 increase). *Double crochet in the next 7 stitches, double crochet twice in the next stitch.* Repeat from * to * until you have 5 stitches left. Double crochet in each of the last 5 stitches. Slip stitch in the first stitch to join the round—88 stitches total.

* Round 3: Repeat Round 2, working 8 double crochet stitches between increases. End the round with 1 double crochet in each of the last 6 stitches. Slip stitch in the first stitch to join the round—98 stitches total.

* Round 4: Repeat Round 2, working 9 double crochet stitches between increases. End the round with 1 double crochet in each of the last 7 stitches. Slip stitch in the first stitch to join the round—108 stitches total.

* Round 5: Repeat Round 2, working 10 double crochet stitches between increases. End the round with 1 double crochet in each of the last 8 stitches. Slip

stitch in the first stitch to join the round—118 stitches total.

* Round 6: Repeat Round 2, working 11 double crochet stitches between increases. End the round with 1 double crochet in each of the last 9 stitches. Slip stitch in the first stitch to join the round—128 stitches total.

* Round 7: Repeat Round 2, working 12 double crochet stitches between increases. End the round with 1 double crochet in each of the last 10 stitches. Slip stitch in the first stitch to join the round—138 stitches total.

* Round 8: Repeat Round 2, working 13 double crochet stitches between increases. End the round with 1 double crochet in each of the last 11 stitches. Slip stitch in the first stitch to join the round—148 stitches total.

* Round 9: Repeat Round 2, working 14 double crochet stitches between increases. End the round with 1 double crochet in each of the last 12 stitches. Slip stitch in the first stitch to join the round—158 stitches total.

* Round 10: Repeat Round 2, working 15 double crochet stitches between increases. End the round with 1 double crochet in each of the last 13 stitches. Slip stitch in the first stitch to join the round—168 stitches total.

* Round 11: Repeat Round 2, working 16 double crochet stitches between increases. End the round with 1 double crochet in each of the last 14 stitches. Slip stitch in the first stitch to join the round—178 stitches total.

* Round 12: Repeat Round 2, working 17 double crochet stitches between increases. End the round with 1 double crochet in each of the last 15 stitches. Slip stitch in the first stitch to join the round—188 stitches total.

* Round 13: Repeat Round 2, working 18 double crochet stitches between increases. End the round with 1 double crochet in each of the last 16 stitches. Slip stitch in the first stitch to join the round—198 stitches total.

* Round 14: Repeat Round 2, working 19 double crochet stitches between increases. End the round with 1 double crochet in each of the last 17 stitches.

Slip stitch in the first stitch to join the round—208 stitches total.

* Round 15: Repeat Round 2, working 20 double crochet stitches between increases. End the round with 1 double crochet in each of the last 18 stitches. Slip stitch in the first stitch to join the round—218 stitches total.

Now crochet the sides.

* Round 1: Change to Ebony yarn. Chain 2. Double crochet in each stitch to the end of the round. Slip stitch in the first stitch to join the round.

* Rounds 2–4: Repeat Round 1.

* Fasten off and weave in the yarn ends.

Back

* Repeat as for the Front, but do not fasten off at the end.

Now make the buttonholes.

* Turn the piece so that the wrong side is facing you.

* Buttonhole row: Single crochet in the next stitch. *Chain 3, skip the next 3 stitches, single crochet in the next 5 stitches.* Repeat from * to * three more times. Chain 3, skip the next 3 stitches, single crochet in the next stitch. You now have 5 button loops.

* Cut the yarn, fasten off, and weave in the yarn ends.

FINISHING

1. Lay the front and back pieces with right sides together. Sew them together using a single crochet or whip stitch, starting at one end of the button loop section and working around the pillow until you get back to the beginning of that section. Turn the piece right side out.

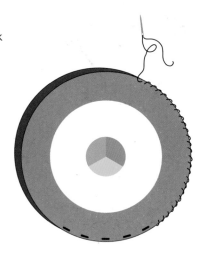

making a pillow form

You will need:

* 2 yards white fabric, such as cotton muslin
* 1 bag of polyfill or Styrofoam for stuffing
* Sewing needle and thread

1. Cut two 13-inch-diameter circles out of the fabric.

2. Sew them together ½ inch from the edge with a running stitch, leaving a 3-inch opening for stuffing.

3. Turn the circle right side out, and fill the form with stuffing. Sew the opening closed.

3" opening

2. To see where to sew the buttons, insert the pillow form and put a stitch marker into the side opposite each button loop as a marker. Remove the pillow insert and sew a button where each marker is. The buttons should go on the last row of crochet, with half of each one extending beyond the edge of the pillow.

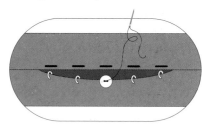

Samantha Scarf

Pattern by Tiffany Roots

SKILLS Chain, slip stitch, single crochet, double crochet, treble crochet, working in the round, weaving in ends

This girly scarf is made up of 17 flower motifs that you join together as you work. Feel free to play around with the colors—there are so many cool combinations you can try!

FINISHED MEASUREMENTS
About 4½ x 76½ inches

MATERIALS
* Lion Brand Wool-Ease yarn (80% acrylic, 20% wool; 197 yds/180 m per 3 oz/85 g): 1 ball each in Lilac [Color A] and Cranberry [Color B]
* 6.0 mm (size J) crochet hook
* Yarn needle

GAUGE
1 flower = 4½ inches across

PATTERN
You start by making one flower. Then, as you make each new flower, you join it to the one before.

Beginning flower
* Using Color A, chain 4. Join with a slip stitch in the fourth chain from your hook to make a ring.
* Round 1: Slip stitch into the center of the ring, then chain 3 (this counts as your first double crochet). Work 10 double crochets into the ring, then work 1 more double crochet, changing to Color B on the final step of the stitch. Slip stitch in the third chain of the first double crochet—12 double crochets total.
* Round 2: Chain 1, work 2 single crochets in the same stitch, then work 2 single crochets into each of the next 10 stitches; work 2 single crochets in the next stitch, changing back to Color A before finishing the last stitch. Slip stitch in the first single crochet—24 single crochets total.
* Round 3: Chain 1, work 1 single crochet in the same stitch. *Chain 4, skip the next 3 stitches, single crochet in the next stitch.* Repeat from * to * four more times. Chain 4, skip the next 3 stitches, join with a slip stitch in the first single crochet. The chains each form a gap, called a "chain-4 space."
* Round 4: Chain 1, single crochet in the same stitch. *Work 5 treble crochets into the next chain-4 space, single crochet in the next stitch.* Repeat from * to * four more times. Work 5 treble crochets into the next chain-4 space. Join with a slip stitch in the first single crochet. Fasten off.

Flower 1
* Repeat Rounds 1–3 of the Beginning flower, but reverse the colors.
* Round 4: Chain 1, work 1 single crochet in the same stitch. Work 2 treble crochets into the next chain-4 space. Now join to the previous flower as follows: Insert your hook through the third treble crochet of the bottom right petal of the previous flower, as shown, and work a treble crochet through the chain-4 space to join the flowers. Work 2 more treble crochets, single crochet into the next stitch. Work 2 treble crochets in the next chain-4 space. Now do a second joining treble crochet, inserting your hook through the third treble crochet of the bottom left petal of the previous flower. Work 2 more treble crochets, single crochet in the next stitch. *Work 5 treble crochets into the next chain-4 space, single crochet in the next stitch.* Repeat from * to * two more times, then work 5 treble crochets into the next chain-4 space. Join with a slip stitch in the first single crochet. Fasten off.

Flower 2

✳ Repeat Rounds 1–3 of the Beginning flower.

✳ Round 4: Repeat Round 4 of Flower 1.

Repeat Flowers 1 and 2 seven more times for a total of 17 flowers. Weave in the yarn ends.

Key Chain Baubles

I ♥ Crochet

Pattern by Cecily Keim

SKILLS Chain, slip stitch, single crochet, double crochet, treble crochet, double treble crochet, decreasing, working in the round, weaving in ends

You can use this basic bauble pattern to make all sorts of fun shapes and creatures! Attach them to key chains, zippers, hair ties, and belt loops. Trade them with your friends or make a bunch for yourself.

FINISHED MEASUREMENT
Each bauble is about 1½ inches in diameter.

MATERIALS
* Patons Grace yarn (100% mercerized cotton; 136 yds/125 m per 1.75 oz/50 g) in assorted colors
* 4.0 mm (size G) crochet hook
* Small amount of stuffing
* Beads, googly eyes, embroidery needle and thread (optional)

GAUGE
5 stitches/5 rows = 1 inch
[Note: Gauge is not important for this project.]

PATTERN
Basic bauble
* Chain 2.
* Round 1: Work 7 single crochets into the first chain. Do not join the round; you will work in a spiral. Place a stitch marker in the first stitch to mark the start of the round. When you reach the marker again, remove it and work the stitch as directed, then immediately place the marker into the stitch you just made to mark the start of the next round.

* Round 2: Work 2 single crochets in each stitch around—14 single crochets total.
* Round 3: Single crochet in each stitch around.
* Round 4: *Single crochet in the next stitch, 2 single crochets in the next stitch.* Repeat from * to * to complete the round—21 single crochets total.
* Rounds 5–7: Single crochet in each stitch around.
* Decrease rounds: *Work 2 single crochets together over the next 2 stitches and 1 single crochet in each of the next 3 stitches.* Repeat from * to * until there are 10 stitches left.

FINISHING
Notice that the two sides of the fabric have different textures. Choose which side you want to be on the outside. Make sure this side is facing out as you start to stuff your bauble.

* Take a small amount of stuffing and roll it in your hands. This helps to keep the stuffing from poking through stitches. Stuff the bauble. (Don't overstuff! Too much stuffing makes it harder to work with the bauble and stretches out the stitches.)
* Fasten off, leaving an 8-inch tail. Weave the yarn tail through the last 10 stitches and pull gently to close the bauble. Weave in the yarn ends.
* You can decorate the bauble by stitching into the fabric you've already crocheted, working into the spaces between the stitches.

MAKING THE PLANET
Start by making and stuffing the Basic bauble. Then add the plantet's "ring" as follows:
* Round 1: Join contrasting yarn to the 7th round of the bauble, chain 1. Work 1 single crochet into the space between each stitch all around. Slip stitch in the first single crochet of this round to join.
* Round 2: Chain 1. *Single crochet in the first 2 stitches and 2 single crochets in the next stitch.* Repeat from * to * around. Slip stitch in the first

single crochet of this round to join. Fasten off and weave in the yarn ends.

MAKING THE FLOWER

Make the Basic bauble, then proceed as follows:

* Round 1: Using the same color yarn you used for the bauble, join yarn to the 7th round of the bauble, chain 1. Single crochet into the space between each stitch all around. Change to the color for the petals. Slip stitch in the first single crochet of this round to join.

* Round 2: Slip stitch in the first stitch. Make a petal as follows: *Chain 2, [double crochet, 2 treble crochet] in the next stitch. [Treble crochet, double crochet, chain 2, slip stitch] in the next stitch. Slip stitch into the next stitch.* Repeat from * to * six more times. Slip stitch in the first slip stitch of this round to join. Fasten off and weave in the yarn ends.

MAKING THE MONKEY FACE

* Follow the Basic bauble directions, working Rounds 1 and 2 in one color and the rest of the bauble in another color. Round 1 will be the center of the face.

* Squeeze the bauble to flatten it for the face. If necessary, leave a heavy book on it overnight.

* To make an ear, join yarn to the upper right of the face. Chain 1 and work 4 single crochets into the same stitch space. Slip stitch in the next stitch space. Fasten off and weave in the yarn ends. Repeat on the upper left for the other ear.

* To make the eyes, nose, and mouth, sew on beads, glue on googly eyes, or embroider the features.

Blossom Belt

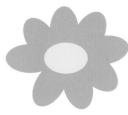

Pattern by Marlo Cairns

SKILLS Chain, slip stitch, double crochet, popcorn stitch, joining new yarn, weaving in ends

This belt is the ultimate! You make the flowers as you go. And it's the perfect project to make with friends—crochet together and you'll all have matching belts!

FINISHED MEASUREMENTS

40 x 2 inches

MATERIALS

* Crystal Palace Shimmer yarn (86% acrylic, 14% nylon; 90 yds per 50g): 2 balls in Ocean Blue [Color A]; 1 ball each in Periwinkle [Color B], Strawberry [Color C], and Celery [Color D]
* 5.0mm (size H) hook
* Yarn needle

GAUGE

9 double crochets/4 rows = 2 inches

PATTERN

* With Color A, chain 11.
* Row 1: Double crochet in the 4th chain from your hook (the first 3 chains count as the first double crochet of this row and throughout the pattern) and in each chain across. Chain 3, turn—9 double crochets total.
* Rows 2–3: Double crochet in each stitch across, and in the top of the turning chain from the previous row. Chain 3, turn.

* Row 4: Double crochet in each stitch across and in the top of the turning chain from the previous row. Chain 1, turn.
* Row 5: Slip stitch in the next 5 stitches. Drop Color A but do not cut the yarn. Insert your hook in the same stitch you just slip stitched in, yarn over with Color B, and pull up a loop. Chain 5, and slip stitch in the same stitch to form a ring. Make one flower as follows: [Chain 2. Work 5 popcorn stitches (see opposite page) into the ring, slip stitch to the first popcorn to join. Fasten off, leaving a 5-inch tail. Drop Color B.] Pick up Color A and slip stitch in the remaining 4 stitches of the row. Chain 3, turn—9 slip stitches total, plus 1 flower.
* Row 6: Skip the first slip stitch from the previous row, and double crochet in each slip stitch across. Chain 3, turn.
* Rows 7–9: Double crochet in each stitch across and in the top of the turning chain from the previous row. Chain 3, and turn.
* Row 10: Double crochet in each stitch across and in the top of the turning chain from the previous row. Chain 1, turn.
* Repeat Rows 5–10, using Color C for the next flower and Color D for the one after that. Continue making flowers with Colors B, C, and D until the belt is the desired length.
* Fasten off and weave in the yarn ends. To add fringe, see page 49.

popcorn stitch

Work 5 double crochets in the stitch indicated. Remove your hook from the loop of the last double crochet you made and insert it in the first double crochet stitch. Grab the dropped loop with your hook and pull it through the stitch, closing up the top of the popcorn. Chain 1.

Friendship Cuffs

Pattern by Even Howard

SKILLS Chain, slip stitch, single crochet, half double crochet, double crochet, treble crochet, decreasing, working in the round, weaving in ends

These fun cuffs are made with embroidery floss, which is available in so many colors, you can crochet a cuff every day for a year and never make the same one twice. Swap 'em with your friends for a more sophisticated take on the friendship bracelet.

FINISHED MEASUREMENTS

Straight cuff: 1³⁄₄ x 6³⁄₄ inches; **curvy cuff:** ³⁄₄ x 6¹⁄₄ inches

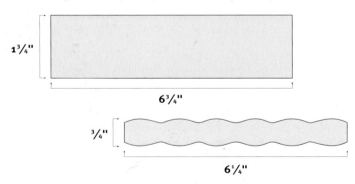

MATERIALS

* DMC Six Strand Embroidery Floss (100% mercerized cotton): 3 skeins in Light Green 3053 [Color A]; 1 skein each in Pale Pink 948 [Color B], Cherry Red 347, Yellow 726, White, Dark Green 3011, Brown 632, and Dark Red 498
* 1.9mm (size 5) steel crochet hook
* ¹⁄₄-inch buttons or beads; 2 for straight cuff, 1 for curvy cuff
* Straight pins
* Sewing needle and thread

GAUGE

9¹⁄₂ stitches = 2 inches

PATTERN

Straight cuff

This cuff is worked from one short end to the other so the beginning chain is the width of the cuff.

* With Color A, chain 17.
* Row 1: Single crochet in the second chain from your hook and in each chain across. Chain 1, turn—16 single crochets total.
* Row 2: Single crochet in the first stitch and in each stitch across. Chain 1, turn.
* Row 3: Single crochet in the first stitch and in each stitch across. Chain 4, turn. (The turning chain does not count as a stitch.)
* Row 4: Treble crochet in the first stitch and in each stitch across. Chain 1, turn.
* Row 5: Single crochet in the first stitch and in each stitch across. Do not work a single crochet in the turning chain from the previous row. Chain 1, turn.
* Rows 6–41: Repeat Rows 2–5. Try on the cuff at this point and add more rows before proceeding if you want it to be longer.
* Row 42: Single crochet across. Chain 1, turn.
* Row 43 (button loop row): Single crochet in each of the first 4 stitches. Chain 14 (first button loop made). Single crochet in each of the next 8 stitches. Chain 14 (second button loop made). Single crochet in each of the next 4 stitches.
* Fasten off and weave in yarn ends. Try on the cuff and ask a friend to mark where the buttons should go with a straight pin. Using a sewing needle and thread, sew on buttons.

more ➤

Curvy cuff

This cuff is worked along its length, so the starting chain is the *length* of the cuff.

* With Color B, chain 64. Put the chain around your wrist to check for size; if you want to increase the length, make 9 more foundation chains to add one more scallop.

* Row 1: Working in the back loop only, single crochet in the second chain from your hook. *Half double crochet in the next chain, double crochet in the next chain, treble crochet in each of the next 3 chains, double crochet in the next chain, half double crochet in the next chain, single crochet in the last chain (1 scallop made).* Continue across, repeating from * to * 6 more times. Do not turn; instead you will rotate around to the other side of the chain.

* Button loop: Chain 12 for a button loop, rotate to work the other side of the foundation chain.

* Row 2: Working in the front (unworked) loop of the foundation chain, single crochet in the first chain. *Half double crochet in the next chain, double crochet in the next chain, treble crochet in each of the next 3 chains, double crochet in the next chain, half-double crochet in the next chain, single crochet in the last chain.* Repeat from * to * 6 more times.

Slip stitch in the first single crochet of the first row to finish.

* Fasten off and weave in the yarn ends. Try on the cuff and ask a friend to mark where the button will go with a straight pin. Using a sewing needle and thread, sew on the button.

APPLIQUÉS

Heart

* With Dark Red, chain 4. Slip stitch into the first chain to form a small ring.

* Round 1: Chain 3 (this counts as your first double crochet). Work the following into the center of the ring: 4 double crochets, chain 1, 5 double crochets, chain 1, 2 double crochets, treble crochet, chain 2, treble crochet, 2 double crochets, chain 1. Slip stitch in the top of the chain-3 to join the round.

* Round 2: Chain 2. Work 1 double crochet in the next stitch, treble crochet in each of the next 2 stitches, double crochet in the next stitch. Slip stitch into the chain-1 space. Double crochet in the next stitch, treble crochet in each of the next 2 stitches, double crochet in the next stitch. Chain 2, slip stitch in the next stitch.

* Fasten off and weave in the yarn ends.

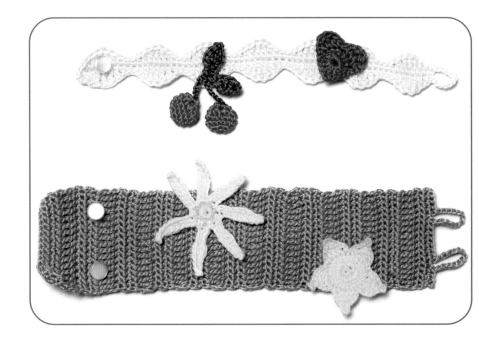

tip

If you want a shortcut, just buy some small appliqués from the crafts store and sew them on!

Star

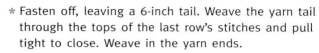

* With Yellow, chain 4. Slip stitch into the first chain to form a small ring.

* Round 1: Chain 4 (this counts as your first treble crochet). Work 24 treble crochets into the ring. Slip stitch in the top of the chain-4 to join the round—25 treble crochets total.

* Round 2: Chain 1. Single crochet in the first stitch, chain 4. Work Star tip cluster as follows: *Yarn over twice, insert your hook in the next stitch and pull up a loop. Yarn over, draw the yarn through 2 of the loops on your hook, but do not finish the stitch.* Repeat from * to * once more, leaving the top of the stitch unfinished. Work one treble crochet normally, pulling the yarn through all 6 loops on the hook as you finish this treble. Now chain 3, single crochet in the top of the cluster (1 picot made). Chain 4, single crochet in the next stitch from Round 1 (Star tip cluster completed). Single crochet in the next stitch, chain 4.** Repeat from * to **, ending with chain 4, and single crochet in the last stitch. Join the round with a slip stitch.

* Fasten off and weave in the yarn ends.

Cherries and Leaves

* With Cherry Red, chain 4. Slip stitch into the first chain to form a small ring.

* Round 1: Chain 1. Work 6 single crochets in the ring. Slip stitch in the first single crochet to join the round—6 single crochets total.

* Round 2: Chain 1. Work two single crochets in each stitch around. Slip stitch in the first single crochet to join the round—12 single crochets total.

* Round 3: Chain 1. Single crochet in each stitch around. Slip stitch in the first single crochet to join the round—12 single crochets total.

* Round 4 (decrease round): Chain 1. *Work the next 2 single crochets together.* Repeat from * to * around. Slip stitch in the first single crochet to join the round—6 single crochets total.

* Fasten off, leaving a 6-inch tail. Weave the yarn tail through the tops of the last row's stitches and pull tight to close. Weave in the yarn ends.

* Repeat for second cherry.

* Now start the leaves. With Dark Green, chain 8.

* Row 1 (first leaf): Single crochet in the second chain from your hook, double crochet in the next chain, treble crochet in each of the next 3 chains, double crochet in the next chain, single crochet in the next chain.

* Row 2 (second leaf): Chain 7 and repeat Row 1 for second leaf. Fasten off and weave in the yarn ends.

* Now make the stems. Attach Brown yarn to the top of one cherry with a knot and pull a loop through the top of the cherry motif. Chain 7. Single crochet through the bottom of the stitch at the center of the two leaves, chain 6, single crochet through the top of the second cherry motif. Fasten off. Weave yarn ends to the inside of the cherries.

Daisy

* With Yellow, chain 4. Slip stitch into the first chain to form a small loop.

* Round 1 (center): Chain 1. Work 7 single crochets into the loop, dropping Yellow and changing to White in the last single crochet. Slip stitch in the first single crochet to join the round.

* Round 2 (petals): *Chain 9, single crochet in the second chain from your hook, single crochet in each of the next 2 stitches, half double crochet in each of the next 2 stitches, single crochet in each of the next 3 stitches (1 petal made). Slip stitch in the next yellow single crochet.* Repeat from * to * around. Slip stitch in the bottom of the first petal to join the round.

* Fasten off and weave in the yarn ends.

Punk Gloves

Pattern by Cecily Keim

SKILLS Chain, slip stitch, single crochet, decreasing, working in the round, weaving in ends

A tame stitch combination turns into a wild, funky fishnet! The yarn's elasticity helps create gloves that fit, well...like a glove!

FINISHED SIZE
One size—yours!

MATERIALS
* 2 skeins Patons Katrina yarn (92% rayon, 8% polyester; 163 yds/150 m per 3.5 oz/100 g) in Noir
* 6.5 mm (size K) hook
* Stitch marker
* Tape measure
* Yarn needle

PATTERN
* Foundation chain: Make a chain with an odd number of stitches that's equal in length to measurement A (see opposite page). Be careful not to stretch your chain when measuring it. Slip stitch to join the last chain to the first chain to form a ring. Do not twist the chain.
* Round 1: Chain 1. Single crochet in the first chain from your hook and in each chain around. Slip stitch in the first single crochet of the round to join. Chain 1, do not turn.
* Round 2: Single crochet in the first stitch and in each stitch around. Slip stitch in the first single crochet of the round to join. Chain 1.
* Round 3: Single crochet in the first stitch. *Chain 1, skip the next stitch, single crochet in the next stitch.* Repeat from * to * to the end of the round.

From here on, the rounds are not joined with a slip stitch but are worked in a spiral instead. Place a stitch marker in the first single crochet in the next round and continue to move the stitch marker to the first stitch as you begin each new round.

* Round 4: *Chain 1, skip the next single crochet, single crochet into the next chain-1 space.* Repeat from * to * for a few rounds, keeping track of how many rounds you work.
* After a few rounds, slip on the piece to try out the fit. It should fit snugly around your upper arm.
* Continue working in pattern until you reach point B. (Remember to write down which round you are on when you get to this point.)
* Now start shaping the forearm with gradual decreases as follows: *Chain 1, skip the next stitch, work 2 single crochets together over the next 2 chain-1 spaces (1 decrease made). [Chain 1, skip the next single crochet, single crochet into the next chain-1 space] 3 times.* Repeat from * to * as many times as needed to get the fit you need.
* Stop decreasing and go back to working in pattern until you reach point C. (Remember to write down which round you are on when you get to this point.)

Now start the thumb hole.

* Chain 1; skip the next single crochet, chain-1 space, and single crochet; then single crochet in the next chain-1 space. *Chain 1, skip the next single crochet, single crochet in next chain-1 space.* Repeat from * to * one more time.

Shape the hand.

* Decrease as follows: Chain 1, skip the next single crochet, work 2 single crochets together over the next 2 chain-1 spaces (1 decrease made). [Chain 1, skip the next single crochet, single crochet into the next chain-1 space] 3 times. Continue working in pattern for 3 to 5 rows, or until your glove covers the palm of your hand. Slip stitch in the next stitch. Fasten off and weave in the yarn ends.

get a custom fit

Decide where on your upper arm you'd like the gloves to start and measure around your arm at this point. We'll refer to this measurement as **A**. Then make note of where points **B** and **C** are on your arm. You will use these measurements as you work the pattern.

As you make the first glove, write down the information below so you can repeat the directions for the second glove.

A = Circumference of your upper arm
# of stitches in foundation chain_____

B = Point immediately above where the arm starts to narrow, about halfway between your elbow and wrist
Do this at Round #_____

C = Point where your thumb starts
Do this at Round #_____

Star Power Purse

Pattern by Julie Holetz

SKILLS Chain, slip stitch, single crochet, half double crochet, decreasing, joining new yarn, seaming, weaving in ends, felting

This purse will take you places you've never been! First you dye yarn with Kool Aid, then you crochet the purse pieces and sew them together. Finally, you felt the purse (see page 82) to make it denser and stronger. If you want, you can skip the dyeing and buy colorful yarn instead—just make sure it's 100 percent wool.

MEASUREMENTS

Unfinished front and back: 16½ x 10 inches
Finished purse: 11 x 7 x 2 inches

front & back

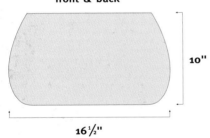

10"

16½"

bottom & sides

2"

27"

appliqué

MATERIALS

* 2 skeins Lion Brand Fisherman's Wool yarn (100% wool, 465 yds/425 m per 8 oz/227 g) in Natural #098—that is dyed orange [Color A] and cherry [Color B]. (See page 81.)
* 5.5 mm (size I) hook
* 8 packs of orange Kool Aid [Color A]
* 8 packs of cherry Kool Aid [Color B]
* Straight pins
* Yarn needle
* Tailor's chalk or pen
* Paper and pencil

GAUGE

14 half double crochet stitches/11½ rows = 5 inches

PATTERN

To dye the yarn with Kool Aid, see page 81.

Front

* With Color A, loosely chain 48.
* Row 1: (right side): Half double crochet in the third chain from your hook. Half double crochet in each chain to the end—47 half double crochets total. Turn.
* Rows 2–13: Chain 2 (this counts as your first half double crochet here and throughout the pattern). Half double crochet in the second stitch and in each stitch across, ending with a half double crochet in the top of the turning chain from the previous row—47 half double crochets total. Turn.
* Row 14: Chain 2, work a half double crochet decrease over next 2 stitches (see page 80). Half double crochet in each stitch across until there are 2 stitches and the turning chain remaining. Half double crochet decrease over the next 2 stitches. Half double crochet in the top of the turning chain. Turn.

more →

half double crochet decrease

To make a half double crochet decrease, here's what to do: Yarn over, insert your hook into the next stitch, yarn over, draw up a loop, yarn over, insert your hook into the next stitch, yarn over, draw up a loop, yarn over, draw yarn through all five loops on your hook. (One half double crochet decrease made.)

* Row 15: Chain 2, half double crochet in the second stitch and in each stitch across, ending with a half double crochet in the top of the turning chain from the previous row. Turn.

* Rows 16–19: Repeat Rows 14 and 15 twice. At the end of Row 19 you will have a total of 41 half double crochets.

* Rows 20–23: Repeat Row 14. At the end of Row 23 you will have a total of 33 half double crochets.

* Fasten off and weave in the yarn ends.

Back
* Work as for front.

Sides and bottom
The sides and bottom of the bag are worked in one long piece. At each color change, cut the old color, leaving a 6-inch tail to weave in later.

* With Color A, chain 10.

* Row 1 (right side): Half double crochet in the third chain from your hook. Half double crochet in each chain across—9 half double crochets total. Turn.

* Rows 2–4: Chain 2, half double crochet in the second stitch and in each stitch across, ending with a half double crochet in the top of the turning chain from the previous row. Turn.

* Row 5: Chain 2, half double crochet in the second stitch and in each stitch across, changing to Color B in the last half double crochet in the top of the turning chain from the previous row. Turn.

* Rows 6–9: Chain 2, half double crochet in the second stitch and in each stitch across, ending with a half double crochet in the top of the turning chain from the previous row. Turn.

* Row 10: Chain 2, half double crochet in the second stitch and in each stitch across, changing to Color A in the last half double crochet in the top of the turning chain from the previous row. Turn.

* Rows 11–14: Chain 2, half double crochet in the second stitch and in each stitch across, ending with a half double crochet in the top of the turning chain from the previous row. Turn.

* Rows 15–84: Repeat Rows 5–14. Do this 7 more times.

* Row 85: Chain 2, half double crochet in the second stitch and in each stitch across, ending with a half double crochet in the top of the turning chain from the previous row. Fasten off and weave in yarn ends.

Strap
* With Color B, chain 3 (the two chains closest to your hook count as your first half double crochet).

* Round 1: Work 5 half double crochets into the third chain from your hook. Slip sitch in the top of the beginning chain-3 to join—6 half double crochets total. Do not turn.

* Round 2: Chain 2, half double crochet in the second stitch from the previous round and in each stitch around. Slip stitch in the top of the beginning chain-2 to join—6 half double crochets total.

* Repeat Round 2 until the piece measures 54 inches (or about 97 rounds). Fasten off, leaving a 12-inch tail.

Square for the star

To make the star, you will crochet a square, felt it, then cut out a star shape to appliqué to the front of the bag. (See star template on page 83.)

* With Color B, chain 34.

* Row 1: Half double crochet in the third chain from your hook and in each chain across—33 half double crochets total. Turn.

* Rows 2–22: Chain 2, half double crochet in the second stitch and in each stitch across, ending with a half double crochet stitch in the top of the turning chain from the previous row.

* Fasten off and weave in the yarn ends.

ASSEMBLING THE PURSE

* Lay the front piece right side down, with the narrow end on top. Now lay the side strip on top, right side up. Pin the pieces together as shown, making sure they are flush along the top edge.

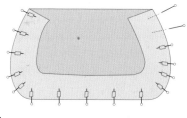

creating color

You can create your own custom colors using, of all things, Kool Aid! For the purse, we used orange and cherry Kool Aid to dye the yarn. To do your own dyeing you will need yarn, one package of Kool Aid per ounce of wool, a large pot, and a wooden spoon for stirring.

PREPARING THE YARN The dye will work better if the yarn is gathered very loosely. So, unwind each skein into a large hank (the opposite of what you normally do!). To do this, take two chairs, such as dining-room chairs, and place them 2 to 3 feet apart. Pulling the yarn out of the middle of the skein, cut four pieces of yarn about 10 inches long each and set them aside. Wrap the remainder of the skein around the backs of the two chairs. While the yarn is still around the chairs, very loosely tie each 10-inch length of yarn around the hank so that the ties are spaced equally apart. This will keep the yarn from tangling too much. Prepare another long hank with the second skein of yarn.

Gently wash each hank in a large bowl or pan of room temperature water with a small amount of mild detergent. Make sure you don't agitate the yarn at all; this will cause the yarn to felt, and you won't be able to crochet with it. Just let the yarn soak up the water and gently stir it around a bit. Let the yarn soak until the Kool Aid is ready.

PREPARING THE COLOR When dyeing with Kool Aid, the amount of water you use isn't important as long as there is enough water to cover the wool. The richness of color comes from the ratio of Kool Aid to yarn— one package of Kool Aid per ounce of wool.

Pour all of the packages of one color of Kool Aid into a very large pot filled partway with room temperature water, and stir until the Kool Aid is dissolved.

DYEING THE YARN Put one hank of yarn into the Kool Aid and make sure it is completely submerged, adding more water if necessary. Put the pot on the stove and heat until the water is close to boiling. Turn off the heat and let the pot sit for another half hour, stirring gently a few times with the wooden spoon.

You'll know the yarn is ready when the water in the pot is clear. Drain the water and allow the yarn to cool in the pot. When the yarn is cool, gently squeeze out the excess water. Squeeze gently so you don't agitate the yarn! Then hang up the yarn. Allow it to dry for at least several hours, or better yet, overnight.

Repeat for each color of yarn.

Once the yarn is completely dry, rewind each hank of yarn into a ball and you're ready to go!

* Row 1: With Color B and working through both the side piece and the front piece, seam as follows: Insert your hook in the first stitch at the upper right edge of the front and pull the yarn through, leaving a 6-inch tail. Chain 1, single crochet in the same stitch you pulled the yarn through. Continue seaming with single crochet, working around the edge of the front, evenly placing 22 more single crochets along that side, 39 single crochets along the bottom edge, and 23 single crochets along the other side, finishing so the last stitch is at the top of the bag. Turn.

* Row 2: Chain 1, slip stitch in the same stitch as the last stitch you worked in the previous row. Then slip stitch in each stitch around—85 slip stitches total. Fasten off and weave in the yarn ends.

* With wrong sides together, pin the back piece to the side piece the same way you did for the front and repeat Rows 1 and 2 for the seam. When you have completed Row 2, keep your hook in the yarn and do not fasten off. Turn your bag so that the top of the bag is facing up, and chain 1.

Now make the same two-row edging around the top of the purse.

* Next row: Work a single crochet in the first stitch at the top of the bag. Working along the top edge, single crochet in the next 32 stitches. Work your next single crochet by inserting your hook through the first stitch of the joining seam and the first stitch of the side piece at the same time. Single crochet in the next 8 stitches along the top of the side piece. Work your next single crochet by inserting your hook through the first stitch of the joining seam and the first stitch of the front piece at the same time. Single crochet in the next 32 stitches along the top of the front piece. Work your next single crochet by inserting your hook through the first stitch of the joining seam and the first stitch of the side piece at the same time. Single crochet in the next 8 stitches. Slip stitch in the first single crochet to join. Turn.

* Next row: Chain 1, slip stitch in the same stitch as the join and in each stitch all the way around. Slip stitch in the first single crochet to join. Fasten off and weave in the yarn ends.

FINISHING

Felt the purse, strap, and square (see below). When they are felted and completely dry, you can attach the strap to the bag.

1. To mark the placement of the strap, use tailor's chalk or a pen to make two small marks on both the front and back pieces. Make the marks 1 inch down from the top and $1\frac{1}{2}$ inches in from the side.

felting

When wool fabric is agitated, it behaves in a funny way. The fibers bond together to create a very dense, very strong fabric that is smaller than it was originally. This is called **felting,** and it's why you are usually instructed to gently hand wash or dry clean a wool sweater—so you won't shrink it! In some cases, though, you *want* to felt a crocheted item because felting makes it superstrong and durable.

To felt the purse, strap, and square, place them in a zippered pillowcase or mesh lingerie bag and put it into the washing machine with a pair of jeans, old sneakers, or tennis ball and about $\frac{1}{4}$ cup of baking soda or mild soap. Wash on the hottest setting but do not let the machine go to the spin cycle. The felting process will take about four to five agitation cycles in the washer, so just reset the washing machine to start over. Check the items after each cycle and remove them when they get to the desired size and texture. Wrap the purse, strap, and square in a towel and roll to remove excess water. If the purse looks distorted, gently (but firmly) reshape it. Stuff it with a plastic form, a cardboard box, or several plastic bags to help it keep its shape as it dries. Allow all of the pieces to air-dry overnight.

2. Take a round, pointy object, such as a knitting needle, and poke through the fabric at each mark, making holes large enough to accommodate the strap. You may really need to put some effort into this, so make sure the knitting needle is pointed away from you.

3. Starting on the inside, thread the strap through the hole in the front to the outside then back in through the hole on the other end of the front. Thread it through the opposite hole in the back, to the outside, then back in through the other end of the back to meet the strap tail.

4. Using the yarn needle, sew the two ends together securely. Fasten off and weave in the yarn ends.

Sewing on the star

Trace the star template below onto paper and cut it out. Place this template on the felted square and cut out the star shape. Sew it onto the front of the bag with a running stitch.

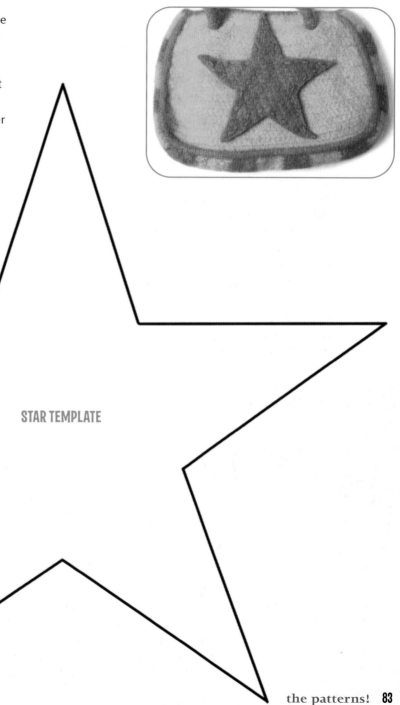

STAR TEMPLATE

Je t'aime Beret

Pattern by Annette Petavy

SKILLS Chain, slip stitch, single crochet, half double crochet, double crochet, increasing, decreasing, working in the round, weaving in ends

A beret can be fun and funky, or classic and stylish. It all depends on the yarn, color, and styling you choose! This pattern will make a beret that fits a 21-inch head but you can follow the instructions on page 86 for making a custom-fit beret.

FINISHED MEASUREMENT

Beret fits a 21-inch head circumference.

MATERIALS

* Patons Grace yarn (100% mercerized cotton; 136 yd/125 m per 1.75 oz/50 g): 3 balls in Marine [Color A]; 1 ball in Fuchsia [Color B]
* 3.75 mm (size F) hook, or size required to obtain a firm fabric
* Stitch marker
* Tape measure
* Yarn needle

GAUGE

24 stitches/26 rows = 4 inches

PATTERN

To make the beginning loop:

* Using Color A, make a loop around two of your fingers, leaving an 8-inch tail (A).
* Slip the loop off and hold it together with your thumb and index finger (B).
* Work the first round of stitches (explained on page 86) into this loop (C).
* When the first round is finished (D), pull on the yarn tail so the hole in the middle closes as much as possible (E). You will be able to tighten this further later, so don't worry about pulling too hard!

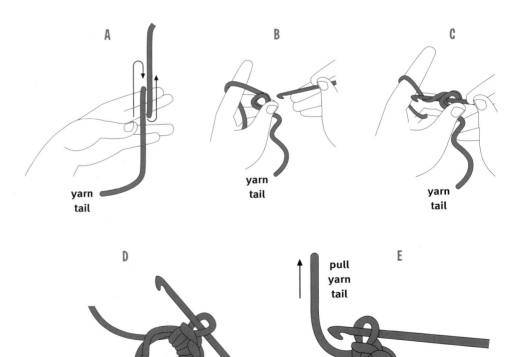

more →

measuring for a custom fit

If you want a custom fit, you'll need a tape measure and a calculator. Measure your head's circumference with a tape measure. You might find it easier to ask another person to help you with this. When measuring a head, the most practical measurement to take is the circumference. When you measure your beret in progress, though, it will be much easier to measure the diameter (straight across the circle). You will convert the circumference of your head to the diameter of the beret using that helpful little number 3.14, a.k.a. pi or π.

Circumference / 3.14 = diameter.

This pattern is written for a head circumference of 21 inches. We figured the diameter this way: **21 / 3.14 = 6.7,** or approximately **6⅔ inches.**

For a custom fit, measure the circumference of your head and then figure out the diameter. Make note of these measurements—you will need them when you work the pattern.

---

* Round 1: Work 6 single crochets in the loop. Tighten the tail as described on page 84. Put a stitch marker in the first stitch (see opposite). Remember to move it up on each round.

* Round 2: Increase by working 2 single crochets in every stitch—12 single crochets total.

* Round 3: *Work 2 single crochets in the next stitch (1 increase made), single crochet in the next stitch.* Repeat from * to * around—18 single crochets.

* Round 4: *Work 2 single crochets in the next stitch (1 increase made), single crochet in each of the next 2 stitches.* Repeat from * to * around—24 single crochets.

* Continue increasing this way, adding one more stitch after the increase on every round. On Round 5, there will be 3 stitches after every increase, on Round 6 there will be 4 stitches after every increase, and so on. After every round there will be 6 more stitches than on the round before.

* Continue working until the diameter of the piece measures about 10¼ inches. (If you're working from your custom measurements, work until the diameter equals your head diameter plus about 3½ inches.) Write down the number of stitches between each increase in your last round.

* Next, work two rounds without increases, working only into the back loop of each stitch (see page 30).

Now you are going to start decreasing. To decrease you work 2 single crochets together.

* On the first decrease round, the number of stitches between the decreases should be the same as the number of stitches between the increases on your last increasing round. If on your last increasing round you had 30 stitches between each increase, you are now going to work 30 stitches between the decreases on your first decreasing round.

* On the next round, work one fewer stitch between the decreases (29, in our example). Continue decreasing like this until the diameter of the opening is about 6⅛ inches. (If you're working from your custom measurements, work until the diameter of the opening equals your head diameter minus ½ inch.)

* Now check for fit. First secure the loop on your hook, either by pulling it out with your hook so it's very long, or by putting another stitch marker in it. Try on the beret. It's not completely finished yet, but you want to check that it fits snugly and comfortably. If it feels too big, work another decreasing round or two, and try it on again. If it feels too small, undo a round and try it on again.

* Once you're satisfied with the fit, reinsert your hook in the active stitch and work four more rounds without any increasing or decreasing. On the last round, work a single crochet in each stitch until 1 stitch remains before the stitch marker. Work a slip stitch in this last stitch, and another one in the first stitch of the round (the one your stitch marker is in). Fasten off and weave in the yarn ends.

Heart

* With Color B, chain 9.
* Row 1: Skip the first chain, single crochet in the next eight chains—8 single crochets total. Turn.
* Row 2: Chain 1, single crochet in each stitch across. Turn.
* Rows 3–8: Repeat Row 2.

Now make the first curve at the top of the Heart.

* Rows 9–10: Chain 1, single crochet in the first stitch, half double crochet in the next stitch, double crochet in each of the next 4 stitches, half double crochet in the next stitch, single crochet in the last stitch. Turn.
* Row 11: Chain 1, slip stitch in the first stitch, single crochet in the next stitch, half double crochet in the next stitch, double crochet in each of the next two stitches, half double crochet in the next stitch, single crochet in the next stitch, slip stitch in the last stitch.

Now make the second curve.

* Repeat Rows 9–11, working into the side of the first eight rows. Do not make the chain in the beginning of Row 9.
* Fasten off and weave in ends. Using Color B yarn and a yarn needle, sew the heart to the beret.

using stitch markers

This pattern is worked in the round without joining the rounds. After working the last stitch of each round, you simply continue with the first stitch in the next round. To keep track of where you are, you should mark the start of every round with a stitch marker, which you will move "up" as your work progresses. Just put the stitch marker in the first stitch of the first round. When you are going to work the next round, take out the marker and work the first stitch in the new round. Then immediately place the marker in the stitch you just made.

Pleated Miniskirt

Pattern by Josi Hannon Madera

SKILLS Chain, slip stitch, single crochet, double treble, dart stitch, cluster, decreasing, weaving in ends

The pattern for this playful skirt is a bit of a challenge—but you're up for it, right? Just take a deep breath, become one with the universe, and go one step at a time. When working on a pattern with multiple sizes such as this one, it helps to photocopy the directions and highlight the instructions for just your size before starting.

MEASUREMENTS
Hip: 32/34 (34/36, 36/38, 38/40) inches
Length: custom fit (see page 91)

MATERIALS
* 6–10 skeins (depending on size) Patons Brilliant yarn (69% acrylic, 19% nylon, 12% polyester; 166 yd/152 m per 1.75 oz/50 g) in Radiant Red
* 3–4 yards of ⅛-inch clear elastic (available at craft and fabric stores)
* 3.75 mm (size F) hook
* 4 stitch markers
* Tape measure
* Yarn needle
* Sewing needle and thread to match yarn color

GAUGE
8 stitches/12 rows = 2 inches

PATTERN
This pattern is worked from the bottom up, in four steps—the bottom edge, pleat, hips, and waistband.
* Chain 216 (224, 232, 240). Being careful not to twist the chain, join the ends together with a slip stitch to form a ring. At the end of each round worked, slip stitch in the first stitch of the round to join and turn the piece before working the next round. The first stitch of each round is worked in the same stitch as the joining.

You'll start with the bottom edge.
* Round 1: Chain 1, single crochet into each of the next 36 (38, 40, 42) stitches, chain 2, skip 2 chains, single crochet in each of the next 16 stitches, chain 2, skip 2 chains, single crochet in each of the next 32 stitches, chain 2, skip 2 chains, single crochet in each of the next 16 stitches, chain 2, skip 2 chains, single crochet in each of the next 108 (114, 120, 126) stitches. Slip stitch in first single crochet to join, turn.

* Round 2: Chain 1, single crochet in each of the next 109 (115, 121, 127) stitches, chain 2, skip 2 chains, single crochet in each of the next 16 stitches, chain 2, skip 2 chains, single crochet into each of the next 32 stitches, chain 2, skip 2 chains, single crochet in each of the next 16 stitches, chain 2, skip 2 stitches, single crochet into each of the next 35 (37, 39, 41) stitches. Slip stitch in first single crochet to join, turn.

* Repeat Rounds 1 and 2 until you have worked the same number of rounds as your custom length. End on an even-numbered round.

Now start the pleat.
* Pleat Round 1: Chain 1, single crochet in each of the next 36 (38, 40, 42) stitches, chain 2, skip 2, *single crochet into the next stitch, dart stitch over the next 2 stitches (see page 90), single crochet in each of the next 10 stitches, dart stitch over the next 2 stitches, single crochet in the next stitch*, chain 2, skip 2, repeat from * to * twice, chain 2, skip 2, repeat from * to * once, chain 2, skip 2, single crochet in each of the next 108 (114, 120, 126) stitches. Slip stitch in first single crochet to join, turn.

more

* Pleat Round 2: Chain 1, single crochet in each of the next 109 (115, 121, 127) stitches, chain 2, skip 2, single crochet in each of the next 14 stitches, chain 2, skip 2, single crochet in each of the next 28 stitches, chain 2, skip 2, single crochet in each of the next 14 stitches, chain 2, skip 2, single crochet in each of the next 35 (37, 39, 41) stitches. Slip stitch in first single crochet to join, turn.

* Pleat Round 3: Chain 1, single crochet in each of the next 36 (38, 40, 42) stitches, chain 2, skip 2, *single crochet in the next stitch, dart stitch over the next 2 stitches, single crochet in each of the next 8 stitches, dart stitch over the next 2 stitches,

single crochet into the next stitch*, chain 2, skip 2, repeat from * to * twice, chain 2, skip 2, repeat from * to * once, chain 2, skip 2, single crochet into each of the next 108 (114, 120, 126) stitches. Slip stitch in first single crochet to join, turn.

* Pleat Round 4: Chain 1, single crochet in each of the next 109 (115, 121, 127) stitches, chain 2, skip 2, single crochet in each of the next 12 stitches, chain 2, skip 2, single crochet in each of the next 24 stitches, chain 2, skip 2, single crochet in each of the next 12 stitches, chain 2, skip 2, single crochet in each of the next 35 (37, 39, 41) stitches. Slip stitch in first single crochet to join, turn.

special stitches

DART STITCH

Insert your hook in the stitch indicated. Yarn over and pull up a loop, yarn over, insert your hook in the next stitch, yarn over and pull up a loop, yarn over and pull the yarn through all four loops on your hook. (One dart stitch made.)

SPECIAL CLUSTER

Insert your hook in the stitch indicated. Yarn over and pull up a loop, yarn over, insert our hook into the same stitch, yarn over and pull up a loop, yarn over and pull the yarn through all four loops on your hook. (One special cluster made.)

DOUBLE TREBLE CROCHET

Yarn over three times, insert your hook in the stitch indicated. Yarn over and pull up a loop, [yarn over and pull the yarn through 2 loops on your hook] four times. (One double treble crochet stitch made.)

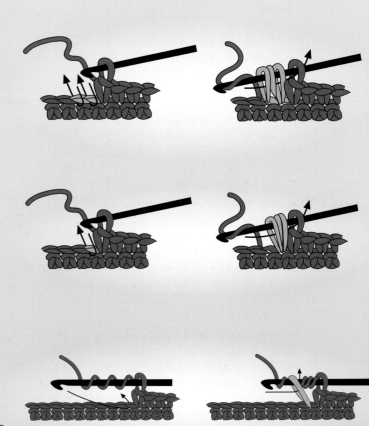

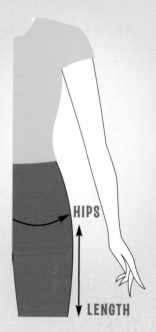

get a custom fit

This skirt pattern is tailored to your personal measurements. Take your measurements while standing in front of a full-length mirror. You may want to ask a friend to help you. First decide how long you want the skirt to be and make a small mark on your leg at that point.

Next, measure around the fullest part of your hips, which is 7 to 8 inches below your natural waist. Round up to the nearest whole inch. Follow the instructions that correspond to this hip measurement.

To figure out the length of the skirt, measure from the same place where you took your hip measurement to the mark you made on your leg. Multiply this number by 6 and write it down. This is your length measurement; it is the number of rounds you will work in the first part of crocheting your skirt.

HIPS

LENGTH

* Pleat Round 5: Chain 1, single crochet in each of the next 36 (38, 40, 42) stitches, chain 2, skip 2, *single crochet in the next stitch, dart stitch over the next 2 stitches, single crochet in each of the next 6 stitches, dart stitch over the next 2 stitches, single crochet in the next stitch*, chain 2, skip 2, repeat from * to * twice, chain 2, skip 2, repeat from * to * once, chain 2, skip 2, single crochet in each of the next 108 (114, 120, 126) stitches. Slip stitch in first single crochet to join, turn.

* Pleat Round 6: Chain 1, single crochet in each of the next 109 (115, 121, 127) stitches, chain 2, skip 2, single crochet in each of the next 10 stitches, chain 2, skip 2, single crochet in each of the next 20 stitches, chain 2, skip 2, single crochet in each of the next 10 stitches, chain 2, skip 2, single crochet in each of the next 35 (37, 39, 41) stitches. Slip stitch in first single crochet to join, turn

* Pleat Round 7: Chain 1, single crochet in each of the next 36 (38, 40, 42) stitches, chain 2, skip 2, *single crochet in the next stitch, dart stitch over the next 2 stitches, single crochet in each of the next 4 stitches, dart stitch over the next 2 stitches, single crochet in the next stitch*, chain 2, skip 2, repeat from* to* twice, chain 2, skip 2, repeat from * to * once, chain 2, skip 2, single crochet in each

of the next 108 (114, 120, 126) stitches. Slip stitch in first single crochet to join, turn.

* Pleat Round 8: Chain 1, single crochet in each of the next 109 (115, 121, 127) stitches, chain 2, skip 2, single crochet in each of the next 8 stitches, chain 2, skip 2, single crochet in each of the next 16 stitches, chain 2, skip 2, single crochet in each of the next 8 stitches, chain 2, skip 2, single crochet in each of the next 35 (37, 39, 41) stitches. Slip stitch in first single crochet to join, turn

For the next round, fold the pleat along the line created by chain-2 spaces by bringing the outside sets of chains together at the center front of the skirt. As you make your stitches in the next round, when you get to the pleat you will work through three thicknesses of fabric using the special cluster stitch (see page 90). When working the special cluster stitches, do not count the chains from the previous rounds.

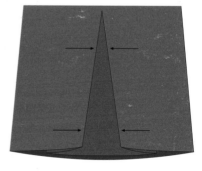

more

* Pleat Round 9: Chain 1, single crochet in each of the next 28 (30, 32, 34) stitches. *Working through three thicknesses of fabric,* work 1 special cluster in each of the next 16 stitches (pleat is now secured). Single crochet in each of the next 100 (106, 112, 118) stitches. Slip stitch in first single crochet to join, turn

* Pleat Round 10: Chain 1, single crochet in each of the next 144 (152, 160, 168) stitches. Slip stitch in first single crochet to join, turn.

* Pleat Rounds 11–14: Repeat Pleat Round 10.

Now you'll start the hip section. You will use dart stitches on certain odd rounds to narrow the hips as you work toward the waist.

* Hips Round 1: Chain 1, single crochet in each of the next 90 (95, 100, 105) stitches, dart stitch over next 2 stitches, single crochet in each of the next 32 (34, 36, 38) stitches, dart stitch over next 2 stitches, single crochet in each of the next 18 (19, 20, 21) stitches. Slip stitch in first single crochet to join, turn.

* Hips Round 2: Chain 1, single crochet in each of the next 142 (150, 158, 166) stitches. Slip stitch in first single crochet to join, turn.

* Hips Rounds 3–4: Repeat Hips Round 2.

* Hips Round 5: Chain 1, single crochet in each of the next 90 (95, 100, 105) stitches, dart stitch over next 2 stitches, single crochet in each of the next 30 (32, 34, 36) stitches, dart stitch over next 2 stitches, single crochet in each of the next 18 (19, 20, 21) stitches. Slip stitch in first single crochet to join, turn.

* Hips Round 6: Chain 1, single crochet in each of the next 140 (148, 156, 164) stitches. Slip stitch in first single crochet to join, turn.

* Hips Rounds 7–8: Repeat Hips Round 6.

* Hips Round 9: Chain 1, single crochet in each of the next 90 (95, 100, 105) stitches, dart stitch over next 2 stitches, single crochet in each of the next 28 (30, 32, 34) stitches, dart stitch over next 2 stitches, single crochet in each of the next 18 (19, 20, 21) stitches. Slip stitch in first single crochet to join, turn.

* Hips Round 10: Chain 1, single crochet in each of the next 138 (146, 154, 162) stitches. Slip stitch in first single crochet to join, turn.

* Hips Round 11: Chain 1, single crochet in each of the next 90 (95, 100, 105) stitches, dart stitch over next 2 stitches, single crochet in each of the next 26 (28, 30, 32) stitches, dart stitch over next 2 stitches, single crochet in each of the next 18 (19, 20, 21) stitches. Slip stitch in first single crochet to join, turn.

* Hips Round 12: Chain 1, single crochet in each of the next 136 (144, 152, 160) stitches. Slip stitch in first single crochet to join, turn.

* Hips Round 13: Chain 1, single crochet in each of the next 90 (95, 100, 105) stitches, dart stitch over next 2 stitches, single crochet in each of the next 24 (26, 28, 30) stitches, dart stitch over next 2 stitches, single crochet in each of the next 18 (19, 20, 21) stitches. Slip stitch in first single crochet to join, turn.

* Hips Round 14: Chain 1, single crochet in each of the next 134 (142, 150, 158) stitches. Slip stitch in first single crochet to join, turn.

* Hips Round 15: Chain 1, single crochet in each of the next 90 (95, 100, 105) stitches, dart stitch over next 2 stitches, single crochet in each of the next 22 (24, 26, 28) stitches, dart stitch over next 2 stitches, single crochet in each of the next 18 (19, 20, 21) stitches. Slip stitch in first single crochet to join, turn.

* Hips Round 16: Chain 1, single crochet in each of the next 132 (140, 148, 156) stitches. Slip stitch in first single crochet to join, turn.

* Hips Round 17: Chain 1, single crochet in each of the next 90 (95, 100, 105) stitches, dart stitch over next 2 stitches, single crochet in each of the next 20 (22, 24, 26) stitches, dart stitch over next 2 stitches, single crochet in each of the next 18 (19, 20, 21) stitches. Slip stitch in first single crochet to join, turn.

* Hips Round 18: Chain 1, single crochet in each of the next 130 (138, 146, 154) stitches. Slip stitch in first single crochet to join, turn.

* Hips Round 19: Chain 1, single crochet in each of the next 90 (95, 100, 105) stitches, dart stitch over next 2 stitches, single crochet in each of the next 18 (20, 22, 24) stitches, dart stitch over next 2 stitches, single crochet in each of the next 18 (19, 20, 21) stitches. Slip stitch in first single crochet to join, turn.

* Hips Round 20: Chain 1, single crochet in each of the next 128 (136, 144, 152) stitches. Slip stitch in first single crochet to join, turn.

Now you'll make the waistband of the skirt, working over the elastic rings. To do this, you'll place one of the rings over the round just worked and work the next round of stitches over it to secure it to the previous round. Then you'll join and turn as usual.

elastic rings

* Waistband Round 1 (working around elastic as described at left): Chain 1, single crochet in each of the next 128 (136, 144, 152) stitches. Slip stitch in first single crochet to join, turn.

* Waistband Round 2: Chain 1, *single crochet in each of the next 4 stitches, 1 double treble crochet in each of the next 4 stitches.* Repeat from * to * around. Slip stitch in first single crochet to join, turn.

* Waistband Round 3: Chain 1, single crochet in each of the next 128 (136, 144, 152) stitches. Slip stitch in first single crochet to join, turn.

* Waistband Round 4: Repeat Waistband Round 2.

* Waistband Rounds 5–8: Repeat Waistband Rounds 1–4.

* Waistband Round 9: Repeat Waistband Round 1.

* Waistband Round 10: Repeat Waistband Round 3.

* Waistband Round 11: Chain 1, slip stitch in same stitch to join. *Chain 1, slip stitch in the next stitch.* Repeat from * to * around. Slip stitch in first chain to join. Fasten off and weave in the yarn ends.

Tie (optional)
* Chain 4.

* Row 1: Chain 1, single crochet into each of the 4 chains. Turn.

* Row 2: Chain 1, single crochet in each stitch from the previous row. Turn.

* Repeat Row 2 until the tie is 72 inches long.

* Edging row: Chain 1, slip stitch into the side of the row you just worked. *Chain 1, slip stitch into the side of next row or stitch.* Repeat from * to * around.

* Sew the tie to the right side of the skirt, using a sewing needle and thread.

Three elastic rings help reinforce the skirt's waistband. To create a ring, wrap a piece of elastic flat around your natural waistline and cut it 2 inches shorter than this measurement. To form a ring, overlap the ends of the elastic by ½ inch and sew the ends together, being careful not to twist the elastic. Make three rings.

Get More Info!

Check out these great resources to learn more about crochet. Also take a look at what's available in your own community. Your local library may have crochet books and back issues of crochet magazines with patterns and instructions. Inquire at your local community center to see if it offers crochet classes. Also check out your local yarn or craft stores. They may also offer classes—if they don't they can probably point you in the right direction. And chances are some of your relatives crochet. Ask!

BOOKS & MAGAZINES

There are lots of other crochet books out there, and picking up a crochet magazine is a great way to find stylish patterns and timely information. Take a look at these:

Teach Yourself VISUALLY Crocheting, by Kim P. Werker & Cecily Keim (Wiley, 2006), has tons of photo-illustrated tutorials for basic and more advanced crochet techniques. I'm biased, though, since I co-wrote it!

The Crochet Stitch Bible, by Betty Barnden (Krause Publications, 2004), is a fabulous stitch dictionary with good photos and clearly written stitch patterns. When you're ready to wing it, this book is a great place to start!

Knit.1 Magazine has tons of crochet, too! Check it out quarterly for patterns in the latest fashions, and news about what's going on in the world of knitting and crochet.

Crochet! Magazine is another good magazine to pick up, too.

WEBSITES

Want to join others who love crochet as much as you do? Find out more on the **Crochet Guild of America (CGOA)** site, http://www.crochet.org.

For more about yarn weight, hook sizes, and standard body measurements, check out the **Craft Yarn Council of America's** information at http://www.yarnstandards.com.

Want to find a charity to crochet for? The CGOA has a huge list at http://www.crochet.org/charity2.html.

Want more information or tutorials? If you do a simple search for terms like "crochet tutorials" or "crochet stitches" you'll find lots of websites to help you out.

YARN COMPANIES

The yarns featured in Get Hooked are just one place to start. Take a look at these websites to learn about other yarns, to see the array of beautiful colors available, to find inspiration!

BERNAT
http://www.bernat.com

CRYSTAL PALACE
http://www.straw.com/cpy

DMC EMBROIDERY THREAD
http://www.dmc-usa.com

J. & P. COATS and **AUNT LYDIA'S**
http://www.coatsandclark.com

LION BRAND
http://www.lionbrand.com

PATONS
http://www.patonsyarns.com

Meet the Designers

These designers rock! Here's a little bit about them. If you want to learn more, search for them online!

MARLO CAIRNS (Blossom Belt) taught herself to crochet in 1994. She teaches anyone who wants to learn the art of crochet. Marlo has an online business in which she sells crochet accessories and patterns.

MK CARROLL (Sushi Roll Pillow) demanded that her mother teach her to crochet and knit when she was about 5, and she crocheted many an odd and shapeless object. She still thinks grownups worry too much about results.

MELISSA "MISSA" HILLS (Beauty Bin and Ring Cave) creates crochet patterns for all ages, ranging from complex freeform bags to kid friendly carrots! When she's not busy running her online yarn store, kpixie, she teaches boys and girls to crochet and always reminds them to be super creative with it.

JULIE ARMSTRONG HOLETZ (Star Power Purse) is a writer, designer, technical editor, and creator of SkaMama Designs. She lives with her family in the Seattle area where there are lots of yarn shops to cruise and she is never without a hook. She is the technical editor and a contributor to *Crochet me* online magazine.

EVEN HOWARD (Friendship Cuffs) is a country girl from Montana who loves to travel the world and see what other country girls are doing. Her designs reflect her life ideals of joy and freedom.

DONNA SCHEUNGRAB HULKA (Beaded Bookmark), who has enjoyed arts and crafts as long as she can remember, is a devoted Maryland native now living in beautiful North Carolina. She is grateful to the many wonderful people in her life who have taught, encouraged, and inspired her to create and design.

CECILY KEIM (Bracelet Baglet, Key Chain Baubles, Punk Gloves), through her podcast, Such Sweet Hands, shares her adventures in life and making stuff. Cecily co-authored *Teach Yourself VISUALLY Crocheting* and contributes to *Crochet Me*. You can also find her demonstrating her designs on the DIY channel's Knitty Gritty and Uncommon Threads.

JOSI HANNON MADERA (Pleated Miniskirt) was born and raised on Chicago's southside. Her perfectionist nature and fashionista roots are obvious in the precision and style of her couture crochet patterns.

ANNETTE PETAVY (Je t'Aime Beret) lives in Alsace, France, with her husband and two children. She works as a translator, and loves writing, gardening, cooking, and crocheting.

TIFFANY ROOTS (Samantha Scarf) lives with her two young daughters and husband in the Houston, Texas area. She enjoys designing fun projects and her favorite things to make are funky, quick accessories like hats, scarves, and handbags.

KIM PIPER WERKER (Chunky Scarf, Fresh-Face Washcloth, Hipster Head Scarf) is the founder and editor of *Crochet me* online magazine, where she publishes hip and funky patterns and articles by recreational and professional designers (some of whom are featured in this book). She loves her job, which allows her to play with yarn and hooks and hot glue all day. Originally from New York State, Kim now lives in Vancouver with her husband and their dog. Her first book, *Teach Yourself VISUALLY Crocheting*, coauthored by Cecily Keim, was published in 2006.

Index